Praise for
Spiritual Boredom: Rediscovering the Wonder of Judaism

"From rabbis charged with enriching the spiritual lives of others to disaffected Jews convinced that Judaism has nothing to offer them, all readers will find much to challenge them, to reorient their search for meaning, and to recognize that boredom is inevitable, dangerous and a true blessing."

–Dr. Daniel Gordis, author, *Saving Israel: How the Jewish People Can Win a War That May Never End*

"Erica Brown, one of the great teachers of our age, addresses the spiritual malaise that infects so many people's lives. She identifies the issue and offers creative and challenging ways to address it. I read anything Brown writes but this book all the more so."

–Deborah E. Lipstadt, PhD, Dorot Professor of Modern Jewish and Holocaust Studies, Emory University

"Erica Brown has achieved what seems like a contradiction in terms: she has written an exciting book about boredom. Read it and you will learn much about attention, engagement, zest, and many other blessings of Jewish spirituality, our best antidote to boredom."

–Rabbi Sir Jonathan Sacks, chief rabbi of Britain and the Commonwealth

"The more stimuli, the more boredom. Erica Brown explores this paradox of the contemporary human condition in her wonderful new book and discovers solutions to spiritual lethargy in the wisdom of the ages."

–Rabbi Sid Schwarz, president and founder, PANIM; author, *Finding a Spiritual Home* and *Judaism and Justice*

"Eloquently gives voice to a feeling of boredom so many of us experience in so many settings, Jewish and otherwise. By 'naming the problem' so well, [it] gives all of us a gift, and an opportunity to work toward real solutions."

—**Rabbi Elie Kaunfer**, executive director, Mechon Hadar; author, *Empowered Judaism: Independent Minyanim and the Future of American Jewish Life*

"Engaging.... Puts boredom and its causes in perspective and suggests dozens of constructive ways of shaping a life of meaning and creativity. You will encounter spiritual and moral insights on every page."

—**Rabbi David A. Teutsch**, Louis and Myra Wiener Professor of Contemporary Jewish Civilization, Reconstructionist Rabbinical College; author, *Spiritual Community: The Power to Restore Hope, Commitment and Joy*

"Re-invents wisdom literature for the modern reader. Interesting and challenging."

—**Rabbi Charles Simon**, executive director, Federation for Jewish Men's Clubs; author, *Building a Successful Volunteer Culture: Finding Meaning in Service in the Jewish Community*

SPIRITUAL BOREDOM

Rediscovering the Wonder of Judaism

Dr. Erica Brown

For People of All Faiths, All Backgrounds
JEWISH LIGHTS Publishing

Spiritual Boredom:
Rediscovering the Wonder of Judaism

2009 Hardcover Edition, First Printing
© 2009 by Erica Brown

Library of Congress Cataloging-in-Publication Data
Brown, Erica, 1966–
  Spiritual boredom : rediscovering the wonder of Judaism / Erica Brown.—
Hardcover ed.
    p. cm.
  Includes bibliographical references.
  ISBN: 978-1-58023-405-4 (hardcover)
  ISBN: 978-1-68336-308-8 (pbk.)
  1. Spiritual life—Judaism. 2. Boredom—Religious aspects—Judaism. I. Title.
  BM723.B74 2009
  296.7—dc22

                                                          2009024375

Manufactured in the United States of America
Jacket design: Melanie Robinson

Published by Jewish Lights Publishing
  www.jewishlights.com

For Jeremy,
who has taught me to count my blessings and
with whom there is never
a dull moment.

The cure for boredom is curiosity.
There is no cure for curiosity.

Ellen Par

CONTENTS

Acknowledgments

To my family: Jeremy, Tali, and Gavi. Yishai and Ayelet, thank you for being anchors in our ever-changing world. To my parents and in-laws: thank you for always being unconditionally proud. To my bubbie: thank you for teaching me how to tell a story and for the miracle that is your existence. To my siblings, those born to me and those inherited through marriage: thank you for crossing the distance and staying connected. To Sol Schimmel, Kathy Beller, Ari Pinchot, and Michelle Halber: thanks for taking the time to read and for your incisive comments. To my colleagues: thank you for understanding that the need to write is not the same thing as the need to teach or the need to sit at a desk and do something else. To my close friends and my worship community: thank you for imbuing all the moments of sameness with routinized holiness. To the Avi Chai Foundation and the Covenant Foundation: thank you for your incredible support of my work. To Stuart M. Matlins, publisher of Jewish Lights, Emily Wichland, vice president of Editorial and Production, Kate Treworgy, Michaela Powell, and the staff of Jewish Lights: thank you for working so closely with me to make boredom exciting and for making it all look so easy.

PREFACE

Boredom is the shriek of unused capacities.

Saul Bellow

One late Saturday afternoon, I lay in bed following a heavy and disquieting nap. I felt bored—that dull, heavy listlessness that does not quite make it into the category of anxiety but does not feel safe either. It was not something you could just wake up and shake off, the way that you take off a wet raincoat when you come indoors from the storm.

My boredom was not simply an absence of something to do. I have four children and a full-time job. I am not looking for activities. Rather, my boredom was a condition, a state of mind that I recognize now with increasing frequency. It was not disturbing enough to be depression but not innocent enough to neglect altogether, and it precipitated a series of personal questions. Was I tired of Shabbat, that Jewish sanctuary in time that has been a treasure in my spiritual and family life, which was now becoming too much of a routine: the prayer service, the long lunch with company, the nap that never feels refreshing? Was my boredom more profound, a previously undetected rejection of the religious lifestyle I myself had chosen? Was this a spiritual midlife crisis? Family, suburbia, ritual, the treadmill of office life were perhaps becoming stale without any natural replacement in sight. As an active member of a faith community, I wondered how many of my friends and coreligionists were also struggling with boredom but too afraid of the perceived consequences to have an honest conversation about a difficult topic.

This dishonesty frightened me. It also inspired me. The awareness of boredom kicked me into a profound search for its causes and its resolution. I alleviated my boredom by making it a subject of research. I set out to understand whether boredom is an emotion, a condition, or an attitude. It seems to be all three. I wanted to know whether boredom has a history. It does. I needed to understand how boredom manifests itself in spiritual life and whether Judaism and other religions have something to say about it. They do. Most of all, I contemplated what an absence of inspiration means to Judaism and how practically and personally I was going to remove the cloak of lethargy from my own religious life. The results of my explorations I share with you in the pages that follow.

I have tried to make this book accessible, to tell enough about a modern-day crisis to engage and perplex the reader without overwhelming him or her in dense Talmudic passages or in heavy philosophical tomes. We need to travel together to the synagogue and the classroom, dropping in on the places where boredom reeks, investigating the undercurrents of unhappiness where they live. This book will also discuss boredom generally and not only in the way that it is manifest in the life of a committed or a "casual" Jew. To aid us in this study, I have enlisted the help of philosophers, rock singers, and Jewish wisdom literature to struggle with you to understand boredom's powerful cultural impact. I did this because I worry.

I worry about boredom. I worry that boredom in spiritual terms is, little by little, corroding the recognition of blessing in our lives, in my own life. It is making us tired of that which holds obvious beauty and mystery. I worry about the lack of opportunity we have to reflect on the nagging psychic diseases of our day, of which boredom is chief, that sap Judaism of its mystic and wholesome benefits. Routinization can minimize the intensity of our learning, prayer, and hunger for wonder and leave us feeling that there is little point in caring. Alternatively, routine can offer a wonderful spiritual discipline. But that takes work, the work that will be discussed in this book.

I worry that even in the presence of that which is lofty and ethereal in Judaism, our response will be, "Been there, done that." We will and many already have collectively turned our backs on four thousand glorious years of Jewish history and survival simply because we do not know enough about Judaism for it to be interesting. And, most of all, I worry that if Judaism has lost its luster and failed to engage us, then it cannot possibly shine for the next generation.

I would not have written this book had I believed that there is no cure for Jewish boredom, that it is a disease for which we are personally immune. For this book to be helpful, it must be prescriptive, not merely descriptive. Together we need to find what lies beneath the hackneyed surfaces of faith and ritual to locate a reservoir of meaning that eludes us. We must journey far and deep within.

Solomon's Spleen
Defining Boredom

1

A generation that cannot endure boredom will be a generation of little men.

Bertrand Russell

It was ancient King Solomon of biblical fame who started us thinking about boredom. In Ecclesiastes, his majestic work of aphorisms and sage advice,[1] Solomon tells us repeatedly that life is not entertaining nor should we expect many dazzling surprises: "That which has been, is that which shall be, and that which has been done is that which shall be done. There is nothing new under the sun" (Ecclesiastes 1:9). Not only is nothing new under the sun; everything that has been will continue to be. We have already anticipated and exhausted all possibilities. What is left is the monotony of the every day, Shakespeare's "petty pace." We inhabit the humdrum of yesterday in the endless repetition of tomorrow. We have a word that sums up this life condition perfectly: boredom. And while King Solomon may have felt that in his later years all new experiences had been spent, boredom is generally considered a modern phenomenon.

Many believe that boredom is the crisis of our age. It certainly is a largely unspoken secret in the Jewish world that is gingerly being whispered about with increasing frequency. Journalist and newspaper editor Gary Rosenblatt does not mince words, however, when he says, "The greatest threat to Jewish survival is boredom."[2] Rosenblatt elsewhere writes that "the sheer boredom of Jewish life," in particular, the way the

1

unboring story of the Jewish people has been communicated, is "as sinister a threat as any."[3] One need not search far and wide for evidence. In one Jewish blog, a woman writes about Passover, "Why is this night so much more boring than other nights?"

Is this woman's holiday tedium in line with Solomon's despair? Hard to know. Yet many Jewish commentaries on our verse from Ecclesiastes above do not know what to make of Solomon's boredom, given myriad hopeful biblical statements to the contrary, such as "Choose life" (Deuteronomy 30:19) or "Serve God with joy" (Psalms 100:2). There is even a Talmudic discussion as to the merit of having included Ecclesiastes at all in the biblical canon, given its somber overtones. After all, if we all took Solomon seriously, "Utter futility ... all is futile" (Ecclesiastes 12:8), there would be little point in living. What difference does one life ultimately make? There is nothing new to experience. Life will proceed with its dull charms, its hackneyed events, and its linguistic clichés.

To hold back Ecclesiastes' pain, commentaries struggle with Solomon's language. Perhaps he meant, "*Sometimes* nothing is new under the sun." Alternatively, another interpreter offers this: Solomon may have been referring to human acts, which are limited in their originality, as opposed to acts of God, which are always original. All of these apologetics do not make it past the critical eye. Perhaps, as some contemporary research indicates, Solomon knew that there is inherent value in boredom; it stimulates us to productivity and creativity. Every once in a while it may even generate originality, something new under the sun.

Identifying Boredom

Etiologically, studying causes and assigning origins, boredom has been blamed for a range of contemporary problems from infidelity to self-mutilation to profanity. We need to shock and to be shocked to feel alive precisely *because* of Solomon's warning that there is nothing new under the sun. But what exactly is boredom? If it is regarded as the cause of such serious problems, surely we must have some agreed-upon definition of the term. We don't. According to psychologist Dr. Bruce Leckart:

> The principal emotional component of boredom is a feeling of uninvolvement, a lack of concentration, absence of motivation, a feeling of emptiness and, above all, no excitement or enthusiasm for what is happening.[4]

The failure to engage or feel moved by something or someone creates restlessness or emptiness; the process of disengagement involves diminishing concentration or focus. Just think back to your worst class in high school. According to Leckart, the signs of boredom are not only situational; they may also be emblematic of certain personality flaws and may manifest themselves in individuals who are:

- Overly concerned with pleasing others
- Prone to worry
- Lacking in confidence
- Dependent on others
- Anxious for security and material things
- Conforming
- Sensitive to criticism from self and others
- Afraid of taking chances or making a mistake[5]

The notion that boredom is both situational and personality-based is helpful, but these symptoms, alone or as a cluster, are both too vague and prevalent enough to describe virtually anyone, at one time or another. We may need a more specific diagnosis.

Boredom can be identified or characterized by a range of emotions and behaviors, from a profound inability to find purposefulness or meaning in existence to a simple lack of interest in one's environment caused by an absence of stimulation. Boredom might describe the feelings of a corporate executive who sits at his desk without interesting tasks and questions his choice of profession, or it can describe the seemingly endless expanse of time on a Sunday afternoon experienced by a seven-year-old with nothing to do (I know—I have one). Boredom counts as its synonyms tedium, dulling numbness, passivity, inactivity, and lassitude. As reported earlier, even King Solomon's wealth, women, and appetite for material gains did not spare him this chronic illness, as he sadly recorded (perhaps even bored as he wrote it) that "the silver cord snaps and the golden bowl crashes; the jar is shattered at the spring, and the jug is smashed at the cistern. And the dust returns to the ground" (Ecclesiastes 12:6–7). All that is beautiful and fragile is not long-lived and returns eventually to its primordial state of nonexistence.

Boredom assumes the right or expectation to be entertained or stimulated by the world around us. Parents, teachers, and managers are expected to provide a stimulating environment for others that minimizes boredom; this expectation sets up the individual in charge of "excitement" for failure and assumes an incredible personal burden of responsibility for the inner landscape of someone else.

The writer Sean Desmond Healy, in *Boredom, Self and Culture*, observes that boredom, until recently, may not have been a significant enough state to garner much discussion (so he wrote a book on the subject):

> Boredom is often used to refer to feelings that are superficial …
> feelings so common and of so little effect that the state is
> thought to be too trivial and banal to warrant any sustained
> attention. This very fact may indeed explain why there has
> been so little recognition that boredom has far more profound
> and destructive forms: they have been concealed or rendered
> invisible, by the apparently inoffensive, even childish, aura that
> has surrounded the word.[6]

Boredom is commonly misperceived as the stuff of childish complaint or a problem externally generated. Environments are boring. Work is boring. A teacher is boring. A book is boring.

The poet Dylan Thomas, however, in an elegant turn of phrase, lays the blame squarely with the person experiencing boredom: "Something is boring me. I think it's me."[7] If we take responsibility for a lack of stimulation, then we will also be more likely to manipulate situations and states that are not stimulating and find, to the degree that we can, a way out of boredom. Personal ownership of boredom can also unearth rich inner resources that help reshape "empty" experiences. More will be said on personal ownership of boredom later.

If boredom is as pernicious as these researchers believe, then relieving boredom must become a chief concern for individuals and institutions. Perhaps we have accepted as fact that many of the central organizations and structures of our lives have and will fail to engage us, and that is all right with us. We expect no less, and life, consequently, delivers on our mediocre expectations. In the words of psychoanalyst Erich Fromm, "One may state that one of the main goals of any man today is escape from boredom. Only when one appreciates the intensity of reactions caused by unrelieved boredom, can one have any idea of the power of the impulses engendered by it."[8] As such, boredom corrodes the fabric of everyday life and spirituality and can reduce wonder and optimism to naïve self-interest. Are we going to let that happen?

Identifying Jewish Boredom

Jewish boredom is the product of situations and behaviors within a Jewish context that are typical, mediocre, and culturally induced. Boredom becomes the bane of communal Jewish living when our friends and institutions stay rooted in sameness. It sums up the tedium of uninteresting prayer services, the humdrum of a Hebrew school class where the *aleph-bet* is taught year after year without curricular sequencing. It is the child who looks out the window of this class and thinks, "Anywhere but here," and reports it to her parent, who only nods with an unstated recognition, as if to say, "I suffered, and for the sake of the Jewish people and guilt, you will, too." It is the Jewish day school student who fails to absorb the sacred appeal of the Bible and Talmud assumed by the teachers but rarely shared by the students. It is the Jewish day school graduate who gets to university and is overstimulated by Renaissance art, the philosophy of language, and an introduction to microbiology and wonders why his Judaic studies have been much less sophisticated.

On college campuses, students are not finding sufficient meaning in their Jewish involvement. Sigmond Shore, founder of the Wake Up Tour, illustrates this in the following:

There is an overwhelming sense of boredom and passivity associated with being Jewish. Jewish joy and Jewish excitement and
Jewish fire are three powerful forces that have not proved integral
to the 90's overused catchword: Jewish Continuity. Students who
are told that they already belong to the most apathetic generation
are all too quick to dismiss yet another agenda devoid of excitement. Young Jews are not clamoring to be Jewishly involved when
they are told, "Be Jewish because your parents are, your grand-
parents are and so many of your ancestors were." Students have
not found reasons why they should be Jewish for themselves.[9]

Students are looking for a fire that they may not be finding. Unlike con-
verts who become Jews by choice out of profound interest or a curious
attachment to Jewish life or the Jewish people, Jewish students and
adults unaffiliated with Judaism naturally think that Judaism is old-
fashioned and hardly relevant in this scientific age. Instead of choosing
to be chosen, they choose to be frozen. They remain untouched by
Jewish life, often ignorant by choice and through childish associations. If
and when they join a Shabbat meal or sit at the Seder table of relatives or
go to a synagogue service, the language of prayer books and Haggadot
feels archaic and distant. A slow yawn swallows them whole, and at
once, they appear lost and disinterested. With no one to challenge them
and little to stimulate their interest, they remain unmoved by Jewish
texts, rituals, and community. Their original assumptions about Judaism
are confirmed. The book that was slightly opened closes for good.

Diagnosing Boredom

Whether your boredom has a Jewish flavor or not is not the ultimate
issue. The question is whether we can expect relief and whether boredom has something to teach us. Ironically, research on boredom is itself
interesting, even though few have truly studied it. Perhaps the study of
boredom can also minimize its effects.

When did we begin to realize that boredom was a subject to be
taken seriously? An English medical treatise published in 1733 con-

cluded that boredom was the result of too much spleen. In premodern medical thinking, the spleen was the organ responsible for depression and melancholy. English poet Anne Kingsmill Finch (1661–1720) wrote a poem called "The Spleen" that bemoans the lowly state of melancholy associated with this part of the body. She called the state produced by the spleen "a calm of discontent." Her lengthy poem, a short piece of which follows, draws us into the state of boredom, both in its physical manifestations and in its emotional resonances.

> *And of her Eyes rebates the wand'ring Fires,*
> *The careless Posture, and the Head reclin'd,*
> *The thoughtful, and composed Face,*
> *Proclaiming the withdrawn, the absent Mind,*
> *Allows the Fop more liberty to gaze,*
> *Who gently for the tender Cause inquires;*
> *The Cause, indeed, is a Defect in Sense,*
> *Yet is the Spleen alleg'd, and still the dull Pretence.*

The withdrawn absent mind, the glazed eyes, the anxious doubts all signal the boredom created by too much spleen. Anne, the Countess of Winchelsea, knew about boredom. She herself suffered depression and described it so accurately in this, her most well-known poem, that physicians used this very poem to describe the problems of the spleen with great clinical accuracy. Anne was not the only one to give the spleen literary importance. The Quaker poet Matthew Green called the spleen "the mind's wrong bias" and called attacks of boredom "spleen-fogs."[10] What is fog but an embracing, amorphous, indefinable, boundary-less substance that, though nothing but air, blurs clarity. Healy writes that these spleen-fog attacks:

> Would be dissipated easily enough ... by a simple bucolic life, one free from ambition and enthusiasm. (Fear of enthusiasm was to the eighteenth what fear of cholesterol is to the late twentieth century.) Perhaps it was for that reason that the English failed to take the spleen seriously, even though some of them were prostrated with what was referred to vaguely as "gout in the head."[11]

Gout in the head sounds funny to us but may be a good way to visualize the impact of living without enthusiasm. Depression is not boredom but may be a symptom that something more serious is on the horizon.

Even Martin Heidegger, one of the most important philosophers of the twentieth century, calls boredom a "mute fog."[12] Whether we call boredom a gout in the head, an enlargement of the spleen, or a fog attack, the idea of seeing it as a medical problem identified with a part of the body must have been to the eighteenth-century mind a source of great relief. After all, one of the frustrations of boredom is not knowing what or whom to blame. A medical diagnosis might come with an intriguing prognosis and medicinal balm, in other words, a ready cure. Take two spleen-reducing pills and see me in the morning. Ah, to think a remedy for boredom could be identified so quickly! What pleasure this diagnosis must have brought to its sufferers.

Today, in an age of too much spleen, we are less naïve than our eighteenth-century friends. We do not assume that boredom can be relegated to one part of the body and be cured by medicinal treatment, although antidepressants are commonly ingested today. If anything, we do not treat boredom as an organ but as an external, contagious disease, of epidemic proportions, that requires the vigilant nurturing of external stimuli to keep it as far away as possible. As a result, we have come to value entertainment far above meaning on the belief that entertainment will kill the bacteria that spawns boredom. Entertainment can stimulate our creative capacity and imagination, but more often than not, it is there as a distraction, a mind-numbing, time-passing distraction. Our collective spleen tires itself out in front of video games and TV screens, walking the corridors of malls and listening to music in ways never imaginable a decade ago.

When I was a child, our local movie theater showed one picture every six weeks or so. Sometimes you saw it several times because there was nothing else to do. Today the cineplex may have twenty theaters and show different movies every week. Thousands of books appear yearly to feed the beast of our boredom and never leave a dull moment. Our boredom reflex is put to the side for the next big performance, yet we will never eliminate boredom through entertainment if it is an essentially internal problem. All of the external stimuli in the world will not take away one bit of it; it will just prolong the distraction so that solutions become more distant and remote.

Ironically, we are not the only ones to suffer lack of stimulation. Eighteenth-century German philosopher Immanuel Kant believed that had Adam and Eve stayed in the Garden of Eden, they too would have suffered boredom.[13] Even paradise was not enough. With few responsibilities, no search for meaning, and no complications, primordial man and woman also got restless. German philosopher Friedrich Nietzsche even claimed that God was bored on the seventh day.[14] Having created so much so perfectly and so quickly, God ran out of ideas. Fortunately or unfortunately, these problems resolved themselves when the Garden became a place of disobedience and challenge.

Legitimizing Boredom

Researchers and authors Teresa Belton and Esther Priyadharshini, in a recent paper in the *Cambridge Journal of Education*, reviewed decades of the limited research available on the subject and concluded that boredom "can be recognized as a legitimate human emotion that can be central to learning and creativity."[15] How so?

Boredom is a judgment. It is an evaluation or a response to an experience, an activity, or a mood. As such, it helps us figure out how to use our time appropriately, how to advise others, and what our personal likes and dislikes are. Boredom is a basic human radar. I will not take this teacher's class again, not go out on a date with him again, not look for work on this assembly line sorting out bad bananas again. My time is so precious that I will not pay attention at this meeting and instead draw swirling tornados all over my yellow legal pad but will do so as discreetly as possible.

According to American journalist and reporter Benedict Carey, in his discussion of the topic for the *New York Times* health section, boredom is an important spam-filter and teacher:

> Some experts say that people tune things out for good reasons, and that over time, boredom becomes a tool for sorting out

information—an increasingly sensitive spam-filter. In various fields including neuroscience and education, research suggests that falling into a numbed trance allows the brain to recast the outside world in ways that can be productive and creative at least as often as they are disruptive.[16]

The brain lapse that we experience when we tune out of an experience may actually trigger creative responses that would otherwise not have developed without that momentary lapse. In other words, we need to be bored so that we can get out of being bored.

Neglecting Boredom

If boredom has worth and utility, then why don't we talk about it more? One of the reasons that boredom scares us, in addition to boring us, is that we know so little about it. As we saw above, there is little consensus about its actual meaning; boredom is used as a catchall complaint to sum up experiences from the banal to the existential. According to Bertrand Russell (1872–1970), perhaps one of the most influential philosophers and mathematicians of the past century, "Boredom as a factor in human behavior has received ... far less attention than it deserves."[17] We rarely examine boredom because our interests often lie in the dramatic emotions: anger, fear, jealousy, lust, or love. Why waste any thought on an emotion as trivial as boredom? Indeed, boredom seems more of an absence than a definable presence; if boredom is nothing, then we cannot say anything meaningful about nothing. And yet, to quote Norwegian philosopher Lars Svendsen, we cannot define boredom because

> we often do not have any well-developed concepts for that which torments us. Very few people indeed have any well thought-out concept of boredom. It is usually a blank label applied to everything that fails to grasp one's interest. Boredom is first and foremost something we live with, not so much something we think about systematically.[18]

Svendsen opens his book *A Philosophy of Boredom* with a personal confession about his own inner state of mind: "My reason for writing this book was this: I was deeply bored for a while."[19] Svendsen's motivation probably explains why you've picked up this book and why I wrote it. You're bored. I'm bored.

But it's not only that we are bored. Those of us who research boredom are doing it because we are *afraid* of being bored. Boredom terrifies us. Boredom within our faith communities scares us acutely. We want to, indeed need to, explain and understand our boredom. We wonder if we will ever feel energized again. We try to calculate how long the malaise will last and what moments of inspiration we will miss. We ask ourselves, if we are being completely honest, am I just bored, or am I losing God or faith because I am not fully engaged? We look around for factors to explain our current emotional state or seeming lack of it. If we are Jewish or of another spiritual commitment, we might look to God or human constructs of religious practice to account for our boredom and might possibly ask, if we are brave enough, is my faith a source of boredom for me? The instant we ask this, to the threatening roar of inner thunder and lightning, we may begin to fear divine reprisal. We fear that faith, that once-upon-a-time source of joy and purposefulness, has outlived its usefulness in our lives.

But hang on. One of the emerging findings in this book is that boredom is important for spiritual living and is rarely a permanent state of mental affairs. Boredom presents us with important challenges. Life is full of cycles. Sometimes we feel completely alive, passionate about what we do or who we are with, loving our work or our studies, feeling deeply refreshed by our leisure and recreational activities. At other times, we feel lethargic and unmoved. We find ourselves trapped in a flat, neutral state that, like a force field, prevents us from connecting with others and being touched by the beauty or blessings in our lives. The philosopher Arthur Schopenhauer observed that, in this sense, boredom is a life condition, rather than a momentary emotion or reaction: "For if life, in the desire for which our essence and existence consists, possessed in itself a positive value and real content, there would be no such thing as boredom: mere existence would fulfill and satisfy us."[20] Mere existence alone, however, does not fulfill and satisfy us.

Mere existence without purpose mimics death for us. Martin Heidegger articulates the sentiment with its most severe consequences: "Profound boredom, drifting here and there in the abysses of our existence like a muffling fog, removes all things and men and oneself along with it into a remarkable indifference. This boredom reveals being as a whole."[21] If religion is the way to sanctify our lives and give existence meaning, then boredom sucks out the meaning we are trying to squeeze out of everyday existence. It is not simply neutral. It is dangerous. If we fail to define boredom or analyze its impact because it is too trivial to take notice of, we may miss the emotional havoc and destruction that it does wreak. If we accept it as a temporary condition, then it can be generative.

Boredom Is New

Solomon tells us that boredom is old. Literary critic and thinker Patricia Spacks, however, contends that boredom is a fairly modern "social construction" that is "a remarkably useful, remarkably inclusive explanatory notion—and a historically explicable one."[22] Boredom is very convenient as an excuse; it sweeps over an entire expanse of activity and reduces virtually anything to a flattened, dull event or emotion.

This expansive, quicksand of a judgment—"I'm bored!" "This is boring me!"—has an interesting history. Strangely, noted American sociologist Orrin Klapp records a rapid increase in the use of the word *boredom* from 1931 to 1961.[23]

> Paradoxically, the new stress on the dignity of individuals may have implied increasing trivialization of experience. As individual life is accorded more importance, focus on daily happenings intensifies. Keeping an eye on small peculiarities has positive consequences but, inviting constant evaluation, also calls attention to the lack of emotional satisfaction in much ordinary experience. The inner life comes to be seen as consequential; therefore its inadequacies invite attention. The concept of boredom serves as an all-purpose register of inadequacy.[24]

When we as a civilization put human beings at the center of life, as opposed to God, country, or community, our own emotional states became more significant to document and understand. Boredom as a record of life's inadequacies and as a summation of the human condition collides with the downfall of religion in Western society.

Monotheistic religions offer an intangible Creator and the possibility of worship. They explore and value what drives the soul. Religion is not interested in making everything transparent. On the contrary, religion places value in a veiled experience of that which is transcendental. The glimmer of truth, the sparkle of that which is lofty and ethereal, touches us from afar and gives us comfort, hope, and something to strive for in dark hours. Modern society has largely taken away that mystery but has not offered us anything substantial or meaningful in its place. And into this vacuum of meaning slipped boredom as a relatively new social construct that has the opposite effect of religion. Nothing is new, exciting, scintillating, mysterious. It's all old hat. As one thinker asks about the human condition today, "The appropriate question to ask about such social conditions is not, Why is everyone bored nowadays? but How has boredom come to be so deeply *assumed* in our culture?"[25] The assumption of boredom is not only a problem of personal hermeneutics. Today it has reached epidemic proportions. It is a cultural malaise often expressed as a question rather than a statement. "What shall I do?" masks the more profound question, "Who am I?"

Back to Solomon

We return to King Solomon's despair and then move beyond it. We know what Solomon means when he reminisces, "Youth and black hair are fleeting" (Ecclesiastes 11:10). We feel it ourselves at times. The fact that there is no way to escape Solomon's sting led to a ritual during the annual reading of Ecclesiastes in the synagogue; the second to last line is read out loud by the entire congregation and then repeated as if to spare sadness as we close the book: "The sum of the matter, when all is said and done: revere God and observe His commandments. For this is the purpose of humanity" (Ecclesiastes 12:13). When boredom tells us there is no meaning, the Hebrew Bible tells us that there is. And the Hebrew Bible makes its recommendations: revere God, observe commandments, love, and give. There is not much else worthwhile. Solomon concludes that it is these acts that confirm human purposefulness.

The same Solomon who wrote that all is futile is also credited with the writing of the Song of Songs, a biblical love song. There is nothing boring in these romantic cadences:

> *Let me be a seal upon your heart,*
> *Like the seal upon your hand.*
> *For love is fierce as death.*
> *Passion is mighty as purgatory.*
> *Its darts are darts of fire,*
> *A blazing flame.*
> *Vast floods cannot quench love,*
> *Nor rivers drown it. (Song of Songs 8:6–7)*

Solomon's imagery is large and explosive, blazing and exciting, breathless and flooding. We could argue that Solomon's insights on passionate love (this biblical book also had a question mark in the Talmud in terms of its canonic status), while interpreted by the Talmudic Sages as love between humans and God, were only natural. Lust is exciting. Yet Solomon was also considered the author of Proverbs, and his praise of wisdom there is no less thrilling:

> *A clever person conceals what he knows*
> *But the mind of a dull person cries out in folly.*
> *The hand of the diligent wields authority,*
> *but the negligent are taxed.*
> *If there is anxiety in a man's mind let him quash it*
> *and turn it into joy with a good word. (Proverbs 12:23–25)*

Wisdom presents possibilities: divine love, material gains, self-knowledge, and friendship. In Proverbs, the wise person knows his course and direction. His heart knows its own bitterness; he understands that there are consequences of his speech and his actions: "Death and life are in the power of the tongue" (Proverbs 18:21). The Solomon of Ecclesiastes found wisdom boring and futile. The Solomon of Proverbs cannot praise it enough.

The Talmud observed that Solomon wrote these books at different life stages. The Song of Songs was the product of his youth. Proverbs was a book of midlife wisdom. Ecclesiastes was a lengthy essay looking back as an old man upon a life richly lived and cynically observed. But this explanation is not the only one that can justify Solomon's change of heart. Nor do we know how old Solomon was when he wielded his master pen. What we do know is that life presents us with different moods and challenges. For some, these happen in the fits and spurts of daily living. For others, romance, wisdom, and pessimism are cyclical and tied to life events, personal milestones, and professional achievements. Thus, boredom is far from a permanent condition. It is a temporary crisis. We must teach ourselves how to ride the wave.

Boredom is also an invitation to revisit our expectations and our responsibility for self-amusement. From a Jewish perspective, boredom, when taken seriously (and we must take boredom seriously), reminds us that we are not making sufficient demands of our inner lives and that our capacity for spiritual growth is being undernourished. Boredom reminds us that it is time to make meaning.

Making Meaning

Viktor Frankl, a Jewish Holocaust survivor and professor of psychiatry, tackles the thorny quest for meaning in his most well-known book, *Man's Search for Meaning*. The book emerged out of his concentration camp experiences, the dark and murky corner of human wretchedness at its worst. Frankl had originally intended to publish it anonymously. He lived to see the book reprinted nearly one hundred times. It has sold more than three million copies and has been translated into twenty-one languages. A Book-of-the-Month "Survey of Lifetime Readers" conducted in 1991 named *Man's Search for Meaning* one of the ten most influential books in America today. What makes this relatively small work so influential?

Frankl confronts the most difficult question plaguing modern man: given the forces of evil in the world and the innate sense of human futility, why live at all?

> Man's search for meaning is the primary motivation in his life and not a "secondary rationalization" of instinctual drives. This meaning is unique and specific in that it must and can be fulfilled by him alone; only then does it achieve a significance which will satisfy his own *will* to meaning.[26]

The search for meaning is not simply a method of escaping boredom or keeping existential angst in check. Meaning is an inherent human need and the primary motivation for existence. We do not avoid boredom through distraction; this only prolongs an underlying sense of rootlessness and anomie. We avoid boredom by actively searching for meaning. Judaism is a powerful compass in that search for meaning and in satisfying this most basic human need.

Embracing the Lion
2
Acedia and Spiritual Fatigue

Boredom is the root of all evil.

Søren Kierkegaard

Jewish boredom is not like other kinds of boredom. Unlike the boredom where we perceive that there is nothing to do in a generalized way, Jewish boredom has specific contexts and triggers. We may experience boredom within a Jewish institution or in the company of a particularly boring group of Jewish people or conventionalized behaviors. We may experience boredom with prayer, ritual, or antiquated methods of Jewish study. Boredom is not merely the complaining yawn of restless children. It is also the slow yet pervasive realization that in place of inspiration, Judaism seems empty of content and meaning.

Within religion, specifically Christianity, boredom has its own challenges and even its own name: acedia. The word *acedia* has been defined as laziness or indifference in religious matters. Think of it as spiritual torpor or apathy, a religious sluggishness that is difficult to overcome. It has been described as a lack of focus, a drowsiness, even as a dizziness within one's spiritual life. Indifference and apathy are attitudes that often follow, a posture we adopt about or toward something that fails to interest us; in a religious context, this can lead to profound disengagement with faith. We may also contribute to our spiritual apathy by layering on cynicism, pessimism, or sarcasm (see chapter 4); I feel disinclined to perform a religious ritual and then, to remove the shame or guilt, act as if the ritual is not important, serves little purpose, or is in itself, uninteresting.

17

Acedia is an important theological problem for a faith that touts the virtues of a monastic life. The lives of monks and nuns are usually dominated by hours of prayer and silence, depending on the religious order. The demon of boredom lurks in such environments. The problem of acedia for the church is not the experience of any of these feelings per se but an apathetic response, a disinterest in repairing the disengagement. Sufferers of acedia should be deeply bothered by its presence, to the point where the victim of its manifestations looks assiduously for a cure. Spiritual boredom is a virus, an infectious *and* contagious illness that must be cured through prevention, early detection, and active amelioration.

The sin of acedia is failing to *tackle* spiritual boredom, which, if not recognized and worked on, can spiral into a host of other attitudes that are corrosive to religious sentiment. As we concluded in the last chapter, boredom is not a problem to trivialize or ignore. Failure to overcome it is called a sin, both because it interrupts a sense of blessing and because it may potentially lead to other sinful behavior to escape from boredom's snare.

How do we describe a boredom that is specifically religious in nature and requires our hard work to overcome, and how is it different qualitatively from any other kind of boredom? Most people do not even realize that boredom comes in more than one flavor. In *Boredom and the Religious Imagination*, Michael Raposa, a professor of religion, uses the word *dryness* to describe this particular type of boredom:

> Temporary feelings of joylessness or desolation are an inevitable part of the spiritual life; these feelings are perceived by most theologians as playing an important, even necessary role in our spiritual economies. They are properly to be regarded as sinful, however, only to the extent that one is responsible for them or demonstrates no real concern about overcoming them.[1]

We need to look no further than the Hebrew Bible to find this arid approach to religion, both literally and figuratively. When the ancient Israelites had had enough of the desert for their liking (three days), they registered their usual complaints to Moses: thirst, fatigue, hunger, weariness. They questioned Moses's judgment as a leader, questioned why God had redeemed them from Egypt and brought them to a wilderness. They lost hope that the Promised Land was within their reach. And, after decades of wandering, their disappointment even couched a certain boredom with complaining itself. Complaining became just as much a wilderness habit as any other.

Their dusty, dry, passionless movement from place to place was not only a reflection of their experiences in the wilderness; it is actually the word they used to articulate their sentiments. After reminiscing about the foods of Egypt, they cry out in the plural, "Now our souls are *dried up*; there is nothing at all, nothing but this manna before our eyes" (Numbers 11:6). Here was a slave group now free, living off divine plenty with daily allotments of manna, who could not experience blessing because of the tedium of wilderness life. They describe more than the impact of the gullet or their taste buds; their very *souls* were dried out. Their eyes were sick and tired of looking at the same food day in and day out. They had a soul weariness that was not dissipating. The problem only got worse with years, worn sandals, and parched throats.

This soul weariness or spiritual boredom had another impact on its victims. Having no recourse to change their situation and perhaps ashamed on some level by their own ingratitude, the Israelites became revisionist historians. Surely they did not believe that God and Moses brought them out of Egypt to die, and yet they repeated that complaint again and again: "If only we had died by the hand of the Lord in the land of Egypt, when we sat by the fleshpots, when we ate our fill of bread! For you have brought us into this wilderness to starve this whole congregation to death" (Exodus 16:3). Their frustration and boredom led them to a fantastical picture of their past lives and an unrealistic assessment of their present:

- They would rather have died in Egypt.
- They sat by the fleshpots of Egypt. They were slaves and hardly entitled to sit beside their masters.
- They ate their fill of bread.
- Moses brought the Jews into the wilderness to die.

They lauded the food of Egypt, unlikely as it was that as slaves they enjoyed the riches of the land. They remembered the fish they had for free, but perhaps their memory failed them. These comments reinforce a typical response to boredom: it generates edginess in its sufferers, who create alternate scenarios where any other situation is superior to theirs, an attitude that stands in the way of making peace with present and future options.

Let's imagine for a moment that Moses would have taken Israelite claims of boredom and monotony seriously, actually acting on them by bringing the Israelites back to Egypt. "Okay. This clearly isn't working out. You're all right. I'm wrong. Let's go back." We would never have made it to the Land of Israel, never have been "a free people in our land" as the Israeli national anthem, "Hatikva," claims. The dire situation in Numbers reminds us not to take claims of boredom too seriously. Sometimes we have to call the bluff of its sufferers. Do you really want to be anywhere but here, even if you are on your way to someplace else? Think about that for a moment.

We can conjure many different outcomes to situations where complaints of boredom are legion and throw entire projects and undertakings out the window. Think of all that would not get achieved if we stopped midway because of tedium. Buildings would never be completed. Children would remain half-raised by frustrated parents. Marathons would not get run to the finish line, and books would stop being written.

A Lion's Share of Religious Zeal

Spiritual torpor or laziness may be internally renewed, but the experience of these emotions does not mean that we do not care about our spiritual "dryness." We simply may not be energetic enough to fight the mental fatigue of acedia. It can be exhausting. We generally expend less energy on an experience of something spiritually new than on the renewed effort to make a habituated behavior meaningful. It is for this reason that the *Shulhan Arukh*, an authoritative code of Jewish law from the sixteenth century, begins with the suggestion that we wake up each morning with the verve of a lion, a fierce, passionate will to make the most meaning of each day: "Rise in the morning with the strength of a lion to serve one's Creator, since God generated the daybreak."[2]

It takes a lion's share of ambition to bring new wonder to greeting each day through the blur of an early rising. Yet, if we are created in God's image, and God re-creates each day, then we need to wake up with a sense of renewed purpose each morning. A commentary written by Rabbi Israel Meir Kagan in the *Mishnah Berurah* at the turn of the last century affirms this very thought: "For such was man's purpose."[3] This same commentary recognizes that waking up early can be a challenge, especially, the author writes, on a very cold day from a very warm bed. It is then that we have to remind ourselves what a blessing it is to be alive and feel gratitude, enough appreciation to energize us and give us the strength to rise and face the day.

The Lion and the Sloth

Waking up like a lion involves exertion. This kind of daily, positive spiritual energy is the opposite of sloth, a disinclination to work or exert oneself, a failure to feel excitement, a lack of urgency. The lion and the sloth are apt metaphors for this range of attitude to daily living, and we might even imagine these two animals engaged in a battle of sorts, which the sloth would lose, naturally, because he just didn't care enough to win. Fighting takes lots of energy.

Waking up with a lion's passion is all well and good for early morning types but a harder recommendation for those who like to lie in bed late, especially on a Sunday morning.

And yet, sloth is the seventh of the seven deadly sins. It is not looked at kindly within a spiritual framework. Where boredom is the problem, sloth is the manifestation. Professor of psychology and education Sol Schimmel posits that sloth or religious laziness

> consists in our submission to the natural human tendency to avoid our obligations when they demand effort and sacrifice. The failure often occurs not because we are evil, but because we

take a narrow view of life. If we could fully appreciate the long-term positive consequences of benevolent behavior for ourselves and for society, we would overcome the annoyance we feel when in acting charitably we forgo immediate pleasures.[4]

Sloth is short-term behavior with often long-term, lingering results. The problem is that laziness is awfully seductive.

The Bible, Talmud, and writers within the Musar movement (a nineteenth-century moralist movement that spread throughout Eastern Europe) understood sloth's inherent and immediate appeal. Ecclesiastes warns, "Through laziness the roof sinks in, and through the hands' remaining low, the house leaks" (Ecclesiastes 10:18). Hands that hang listlessly do not stop up holes in the ceiling. It begins to rain inside.

Life's stable anchors, our homes, our families, and our jobs require a degree of attentive watchfulness. It is not enough to create or build something; it must be actively maintained or it will gradually collapse or disintegrate over time. The pull of entropy is a powerful force working against us in many physically and mentally beguiling ways. Proverbs tells us just how this force works: "A little sleep, a little slumber, a little folding of the hands to sleep and your poverty is suddenly upon you and your want as an armed man" (Proverbs 6:10–11). On the surface, the subject of this admonition did nothing wrong. Little by little he or she caved into the powerful grip of sleep.

We all recognize the incremental magnetic force of sleep, but suddenly we find that sleep overtakes us like a mugging, as if an armed man has taken away something valuable from us, and we are left impoverished. The object that was taken was our will to be active, to grab at life, to feel alive and passionate. The poverty we are left with is none other than the poverty of imagination, the poverty of inactivity, the poverty of wasted time. Giving in to sleep on a frosty morning under the warmth of a down blanket looked logical at the time. Waking up and looking back at the wasted time, however, makes the loss suddenly feel intense.

Deuteronomy, too, speaks loudly to this loss: "Your life shall hang in doubt before you. You will fear day and night and have no affirmation of your life. In the morning you will say, "I wish it were evening." In the evening, you will say, "I wish it were morning" (Deuteronomy 28:66–67). Days go by without meaning. Life is just biding time from morning to evening without purpose.

The prominent Italian rabbi and philosopher Moshe Hayyim Luzzatto (1707–46) during his brief lifetime wrote one of the most well-read Jewish texts of self-improvement, *The Path of the Just*. He warns us of the corrosive effects of laziness, a kind of spiritual illness that takes over in such incremental degrees that we do not always recognize its grip:

> The evil of the lazy man does not come all at once, but little by little, without his recognizing and sensing it. He is pulled from evil to evil until he finds himself sunk in evil's very depths. He begins by not expending the amount of effort which could be expected of him.... This neglect is due not to an inadequate recognition of his duty nor to any other cause, but the increasing weight of his laziness upon him....[5]

In other words, we must be continually alert to the moral entropy that brings about laziness, even when we know rationally that industry will help us achieve more and feel better about ourselves.

The Lion Is Back

When it comes to fighting the powerful forces of sloth, we turn back to our friend, king of the jungle. An ancient Rabbinic midrash, or commentary, again uses lion imagery to wonderful effect to show the impact of religious sloth and the prize of knowing what you should do and avoiding it. Pay attention to the marvelous dialogue:

> They tell the sloth, "Your teacher is in a nearby city. Go and learn Torah from him."
>> He responds, "I fear a lion on the highway."
>> "Your teacher is in your own city."
>> "I fear a lion in the streets."
>> "Your teacher is in your home."

"I am afraid a lion is inside."

"Your teacher is in a room inside your home."

"I am afraid that if I rise from bed, the door will be locked."

"But the door is open."

"I need a little more sleep."[6]

The sloth in this passage is a religious man who even has his own teacher but finds himself drawn into the dangers of inattention and disinterest. He continually finds an excuse to avoid study. The lion that he fears appears as a metaphor for the passion that he lacks. Even knowing that this force occupies the same physical space as he does and the big cat's inherent dangers (it is a lion, after all), our friend is still willing to give into the quicksand that is sloth. The door is wide open to the lion within to change and seek meaning, but he will not take advantage of this open door. He craves more sleep.

Attention Surplus Disorder

American author and philosopher Susan Sontag once complained that she suffered from attention surplus disorder.[7] She noticed and paid attention to everything, too many things. Sontag may represent an extreme in "lioness" behavior even as she touches on the nerve of meaning. Human beings want to be productive; we are naturally curious. We desire personal growth. Carleton Parker, a professor of economics, believes that we are not inherently lazy but innately industrious. Where laziness exists, it is an artificial habit, inculcated by civilization. Humans, he writes, feel a "dignity of labor." Whatever drives them to squander time is not inherent. "It is the job and the industrial environment that produce the slacker, and not the laborer's willful disposition."[8] And when it comes to the inner life in particular, we want to pay attention, even if we can't always focus our minds and hearts properly.

Spiritual boredom is usually the opposite, a neglect to notice anything of interest. Our religious battle between the lion and the sloth is the tension of the inner life played out in the animal kingdom. Boredom appears so often in the guise of laziness for a very simple reason. If it is laziness, then it's my problem; if it is boredom, then I can blame something external like a teacher, a bad job, or a dull relative. The lack of drive or will is our own responsibility; boredom must be about someone or something else, a convenient excuse when we're afraid to look in the mirror.

That boredom is bound to be part of a cerebral life of prayer and contemplation is no surprise; the mind is easily distracted and loss of focus is inevitable when mental demands to achieve higher consciousness are difficult to sustain. Routine habits that anchor ritual observance can easily lose their spiritual patina from overuse, much like worn carpet on a set of well-trodden stairs.

Raposa, who got us started on this discussion, gets to the heart of spiritual attention deficit disorder:

> The bored person has a great deal of difficulty paying attention. Since meditation is, in a sense, the practice of paying attention, it is easy to understand why boredom is such an important problem in the spiritual life.... I can use my imagination to defeat boredom. My ability to do so, however, is not unequivocally a good thing. The imagination itself is perceived by spiritual writers both as an aid to religious insight and as a powerful source of distractions. Here, again, control is an important factor.[9]

As we stated earlier, what constitutes sin is the failure of individuals to take responsibility for overcoming religious boredom. But, as the above quotation illustrates, the use of the imagination to overcome boredom can present its own set of religious problems. What if the images I conjure to avoid boredom in the sanctuary or the boardroom, the classroom or the dining room are themselves dangerous or distracting? We are warned to exhibit self-control when it comes to the imagination, but nothing seems harder when faced with the blankness of empty time as we sit in an uncomfortable pew and listen to a sermon that never seems to end. Minds wander out of the seats and far away. How can we force our minds to do otherwise?

The Lion as Teacher

This is where we invite our lion back for some religious instruction. I learned from Natan Slifkin, the Zoo Rabbi, that only lions in the family of big cats have a name for themselves as a group: a pride. Tigers, panthers, cougars, and the other big cats do not have a group name because their killer instincts are so great that they cannot live in clusters. Thus, they lack a name as a group. The lion, truly one of the fiercest of the big cats, has something that the other big cats lack: self-control. The lion lives in a social web because he can exhibit the self-control not to eat his friends. This notion of strength is embodied in the famous saying "Who is strong? One who controls his desire" (*Pirkei Avot* [Ethics of the Fathers] 4:1). If the lion can have this degree of self-control, then perhaps it is not too much to ask that we control our imaginations when we find our minds wandering. A disciplined mind is a religious boon and a personal help for all of those moments when we, too, would like to eat our friends for dinner.

3 The Hermeneutics of Boredom

> People who decline organized activities are deserters from the great common struggle against boredom.
>
> *Milan Kundera,* Identity

When we believe that something is destined to be boring, we often make sure that it lives up to expectations: a spouse's holiday party, a textbook on the history of Icelandic fish farming, a documentary about the tsetse fly. All of these could actually be fascinating, but we may not give them a chance. We decide early on not to like them.

A single woman has a blind date on Tuesday night. Monday night she hears from a friend how awfully uninteresting he is and how badly he dresses. She does not cancel the date because she has not had a good meal in days. As she sits, eating her fettuccini alfredo with gusto, she imagines herself with someone else in expensive Italian loafers and thus pays no attention to what her date says. She may even have liked him had she given him the time of day. When she reviews the date later on the phone with the same friend, she sums up the evening, "I've never met someone more boring."

Before we even step into a synagogue, work event, or family occasion, we may cloud and freight the experience with negative expectations. Then we confirm our predictions afterward. These judgments may be overcome by a change of attitude, a surprising jilt, or a turn of events during the actual moment, or they may never change because the expectation of boredom is too strong. Alternatively, the synagogue service, the date, and the work party may really be boring, and there is simply nothing we can do about it but roll our eyes and smile nicely to passersby until we can leave.

There is a name for an expectation that colors our interpretation: hermeneutics. *Hermeneutics* is a big word with significant meaning for any discussion of boredom. It refers to theories of interpretation, how we read texts, and how we interpret people. We are constantly engaged in interpretation, "reading" human interactions, investigating speeches and written words for what they really mean. Often, we read interactions with a "hermeneutics of suspicion." The French philosopher Paul Ricoeur (1913–2005) described the hermeneutics of suspicion as "a method of interpretation which assumes that the literal or surface-level meaning of a text is an effort to conceal the political interests which are served by the text. The purpose of interpretation is to strip off the concealment, unmasking those interests."[1] In other words, you hear something other than what a person says and you interpret the words without generosity. You said you were sorry, but you didn't mean it.

We are always involved in a process of interpretation of both the verbal and the written word, and when we suspect that words, texts, or actions are politically loaded or agenda based, we are suspicious. We doubt them. We impugn motives that may or may not be present. A politician makes a promise about education while speaking to a teachers' union. The words are captivating, but on further evaluation and teacher gossip, the politician's presentation was riddled with holes that are filled in with doubts, questions, and unflattering information about similar past promises. At first, we engage in a surface understanding of content, and then we deal with its significance and context, the agendas hidden in the implicit messaging, rather than the explicit articulation. There is reading the lines and then reading between the lines. The latter we call hermeneutics.

According to the philosopher Ruel Pepa, the hermeneutics of suspicion "unmasks and unveils untenable claims."[2] We call someone's bluff. In the words of both of these scholars, the idea of interpretation is a peeling off of the skin or surface layer to see what lies beneath that has gone unwritten or unspoken, the subterranean levels of meaning that elude us. Training in the hermeneutics of suspicion can help an individual question his or her interpretive reality and the system that produced it.

Boredom also has a hermeneutic history. We did not wake up one day and simply interpret events or people as boring. Patricia Spacks, the literary scholar we met earlier, reminds us that boredom is a social construction, late in its development:

> Boredom's status as a cultural construct becomes increasingly apparent as its verbal records multiply. It was born in the same era as the ideas of "leisure" and the pursuit of happiness, and its social and literary functions have charted the development of civilization's discontents.[3]

I would like to borrow this expression and substitute in place of "suspicion" the word *boredom* to suggest a parallel, alternate view of interpretation: "the hermeneutics of boredom." This suggests a method of interpretation where beneath the surface of any given activity is an assumption of tedium or a presumed assumption of boredom before the experience of an event or emotion. Spacks again assists us: "The idea that all activity responds to boredom's threat—such hypotheses depend on the belief in boredom as a universal, like fear and desire. Like fear and desire, it possesses interpretive force … it can generate discourse."[4] Or it can stop discourse.

We close ourselves up to the possibility of being moved or interested because we presume boredom. Presumed boredom, in many ways, is more problematic than actual boredom because it takes up more psychic energy and space than on-the-spot boredom. It also corrupts an experience so that even if it were to prove exciting, participants will experience little stimulation because they have already created a force field to protect them from having an emotional range of response. Let's move from our blind date to how the hermeneutics of boredom might work in a middle school setting.

Mrs. Miller's seventh grade science class is scheduled to go on a field trip to the local museum of natural history at the end of the month.

When Mrs. Miller announces the trip, there is a chorus of moans from the back of the classroom. In terms of individual responses, a child who assumes that a field trip to this museum will be, by its nature, boring will miss potentially remarkable displays right in front of his eyes. Joey, a seventh grader, assumes boredom, and this assumption begins long before the hot, hour-long ride on a yellow school bus into town or his standing before a glass display case of fossilized dinosaur teeth. As soon as the trip is announced, Joey's classmates rate it. Many of them discuss it over the phone several times, emphasizing how "interesting" it will be and commenting on the fascinating stuffed polar bear exhibit.

Joey has been told by peers and other students who went in previous years that he *will* be bored; consequently, boredom is inescapable. Our friend does not want to prepare for an experience other than boredom because, if he were to do that, he would be going against the express expectations and views of others in his peer group, and peer pressure can exert an even stronger pull on children and adolescents than boredom. The night before the trip, Joey asks his mother for better than usual snacks in his lunch to compensate for the preconceived boredom and to focus the conversation on the long, hot bus trip.

Uniformity of interpretation is more important to our little friend than having an experience of intellectual curiosity or entertainment that will set him apart from his friends. He is not willing, under any circumstances, to sit with the four-eyed group at the front of the bus, who have brought healthy snacks, who can't wait to get there. Instead, Joey will point out a particularly dull exhibit or explanation placard, roll his eyes, and give a friend a shared nod of recognition. This will place him in good social standing with peers. Unfortunately, he misses the intriguing fact that there are no polar bears to be found at either pole and that they can swim four miles an hour for up to forty miles in an open sea without resting.

We can now see where this conversation is going. Hermeneutics as a way of interpreting reality is powerful precisely because a good case can be made that perception becomes reality, even if there are other alternatives. The hermeneutics of boredom generates more boredom and prolonged boredom because it shapes experiences that are rarely allowed to prove themselves otherwise. Can we imagine for a second that our friend Joey, the reluctant museum-goer, will actually, at some point during the morning, stop, read the polar bear facts, and turn to his best friend and say, "You should read this. Polar bears are really much more interesting than I thought!"? No, we cannot.

The day could be redeemed of its presumed boredom by some other unanticipated event taking place like a holdup in the museum gift shop or a spectacular bout of throwing up from the most beautiful girl in the class on the bus ride home. When Mom asks, "How was the museum, dear?" Joey can then respond, "Awesome. A guy in a black leather jacket with a stocking over his head got fifty dollars from the museum gift shop before the guards caught him," an experience that was not tied to the educational value of the trip at all. The museum trip, for all of its cost and loss of classroom time, will just become one of a series of school rituals that have virtually no impact on our children.

Reading, Writing, and Mental Fighting

Generally speaking, *hermeneutics* is a philosophical term that helps us understand the relationship between the writer, the reader, and a text that both of them share. Within religion, hermeneutics is a system by which theological texts are to be understood. We Jews have a set of Talmudic hermeneutic principles by which we deconstruct and interpret biblical verses to extract Jewish law. Through hermeneutics, the Sages of the Talmud understood that tefillin, phylacteries, which we are commanded to wear in the central prayer of the *Shema*, are to have black straps, be worn on the forehead and arm, contain certain prayers inside them, and so on. These details are nowhere present in the biblical text. Through a predefined system of interpretative principles, not too different in method from geometry's axioms but not provable empirically, these Talmudic Rabbis set about embellishing one biblical verse and arrived at what they understood the commandment to wear tefillin would actually look like. Without the hermeneutic principles and their use by our ancient Rabbis, we would have little idea what traditional

Jewish rituals would involve because of the economy of words in the Hebrew Bible.

Hermeneutics extends, however, far beyond the Bible, which is a natural locus of interpretive genius; in literature, it plays an important role in literary theory and criticism. In terms of boredom, hermeneutics can entangle the meaning of any page of text. We as readers enter an agreement with a writer. You don't bore me, and I will continue to read what you write. "The ideal dynamic between writing and reading depends in part on boredom as displaced, unmentioned and unmentionable possibility."[5] The writer must assume that the reader will be bored and must engage the reader immediately. Or else. Or else, what? We won't buy the book. Everything about the book's cover, the title, the blurbs, the background of the author, the graphic appeal screams, "Read me. I will fascinate you."

The writer makes an assumed interpretive bargain with the reader. I promise to write something that will entertain you, and you will purchase and read my book to be entertained because we are both in the same business: avoiding psychic entropy. The reader brings both her assumptions and her emotions into what she reads. The English novelist and literary critic A. S. Byatt, in her novel *Possession*, uses a number of digressions to explain the process of interpretation that influences the way that we read. "There are personal readings, which snatch for personal meanings, I am full of love, or disgust or fear, I scan for love or disgust or fear. There are—believe it—impersonal readings—where the mind's eye sees the lines move onwards and the mind's ear hears them sing and sing."[6] Our moods influence our reading and, in turn, influence our understanding of what we read, whether or not we are aware of this at the time. Ultimately, the story of reading is also one of self-understanding.

French author and critic Marcel Proust believed that the act of reading is an intimate act of self-knowledge:

> In reality, every reader is, while he is reading, the reader of his own self. The writer's work is merely a kind of optical instrument he offers to the reader to enable him to discern what, without this book, he would perhaps never have experienced

in himself. And the recognition by the reader in his own self of what the book says is the proof of its veracity.[7]

Reading boring books is critical to self-understanding. In *The Consolations of Philosophy*, philosopher Alain de Botton redeems boredom by suggesting that adopting a critical, "impress me" approach to what we read is important in choosing books wisely and not settling for that which is flat or unenthralling:

> Carefully used, boredom can be a valuable indicator of the merit of books ... taking our levels of boredom into account can temper an otherwise excessive tolerance for balderdash. Those who do not listen to their boredom when reading, like those who pay no attention to pain, may be increasing their suffering unnecessarily. Whatever the dangers of being wrongly bored, there are as many pitfalls in never allowing ourselves to lose patience with our reading matter.[8]

With each page, we judge the author's ability to hold our attention and choose to read further.

Clock-Induced Boredom

Lars Svendsen, our philosopher friend from an earlier chapter, understands the hermeneutics of boredom a little bit differently; he describes it as the way in which we interpret time.[9] We look at our watches because we are bored and then become increasingly bored as the lapse of time grows interminably long. Svendsen makes an important distinction between boredom that is anticipatory and boredom that is situational. Boredom in an airport, to cite his example, is harder to bear than situational boredom because it represents the anticipation or waiting until something *really* happens, like we board a plane to fly somewhere thrilling.[10] We know that we will be bored during certain transitional times because we are only there to prepare for something better. What happens, however, when that something better is not a function of time, as Svendsen would have it, but is about the expectation that nothing exciting could happen so that nothing exciting does happen? That's true even if airports are great places to read, watch people, find out what's fashionable in luggage, or dream about a fantasy escape to Borneo.

Neither situational boredom nor anticipatory boredom is the same as "lifestyle boredom." One psychologist understands this term to mean that your very life isn't working for you anymore:

> Characteristically, some aspect of your style of living no longer gives you the basic gratification, excitement and involvement that it originally produced. In short, you have outgrown your life and failed to notice it. Your job, marriage, location, friends, values, goals or beliefs no longer create a sense of drama, intrigue and involvement.... The bored person also feels that, although there's no point in doing what he's doing, there are really no other viable, attractive alternatives to it. This kind of boredom feeds on itself and for some people, becomes a chronic condition. "That's life," they'll say or, "I guess I'll have to learn to live with it." Eventually, they forget that this is *not* necessarily the human condition.[11]

The "I'll have to live with it" chronic condition of setting expectations too low can negatively influence our professional and personal lives. Lifestyle boredom can place unnecessary limits on what people can or are willing to do. At some level, people can convince themselves that they cannot accomplish what they want or that doing a particular thing is "not me," while at another level, they would very much like to have that experience.[12] Thus, we begin to see how the hermeneutics of boredom work and just how hard it is to fight against.

Whether we anticipate a boredom that may or may not occur, expect boredom because we are entering a dead-man's zone of nothingness on the way to somethingness (like waiting for a flight), or facing lifestyle boredom, all three are largely a function of interpretation and how much our minds influence what is about to happen, what is happening, and what already happened.

Jewish Hermeneutics of Boredom and the Text of Life

So how do we unpack these complex notions of interpretation into an understanding of the hermeneutics of boredom and its relationship to Judaism? Have patience. We can all agree that interpretation is a very basic human function. We do it almost unconsciously but do it best when we are fully alert and attentive readers of the text called life.

The assumed boredom approach to experience hurts Judaism enormously because we close ourselves *off* before opening ourselves *up* to the enormous pleasures of ritual, community, and compassion that Judaism provides in such abundance. Watch Jewish people walk into a synagogue for a family affair who have little experience of its patterns and collective movements. If they are Jewish, they will often talk, gesticulate, yawn, squirm. They simply do not know what to do, so they distract themselves by playing with their jewelry or reading the shul news, even though they don't recognize any of the names or really care. Imagine these same individuals walking into a house of faith belonging to another religion, sitting with reverence and curiosity, wondering what will happen next, or wanting an explanation of every new ritual.

People may be equally ignorant of someone else's faith practices as they are of their own, but someone else's always feels more interesting somehow. On a surface level, they react this way because they assume that limited acquaintance with their own faith and ethnicity is sufficient enough to pass judgment. On a deeper level, this enables people to maintain the status quo of their own lifestyle choices. If they took an interest in what they were experiencing, it might demand lifestyle changes that they are not prepared to make. After all, this is not someone else's faith; it is their own. It must not be taken seriously lest it be taken seriously. In this comfortable state of mental closure, even experiences that may possibly spark interest are quickly dampened.

Judaism, at its best, creates islands of sanctity in time and space. It answers the question, "What shall I do?" through a system of commandments that demand introspection, social action, and divine service, all answering the real question, "Who am I?" Expressed differently, Judaism addresses lifestyle boredom by answering "How shall I live?" Boredom as a cultural assumption of the human condition is simply not helping us advance, progress, squeeze meaning out of our limited existence, and find satisfaction. A hermeneutic of boredom where everything is assumed to be tedious until proven otherwise is problematic for all faiths; arguably, it's most problematic for Judaism because deed is just as important as creed. We answer the question of who we are by what goodness we do in the world.

Restlessness

What happens when we cannot answer these basic existential questions? Irwin Edman (1896–1954) was a Jewish American philosopher, poet, and writer. He explored tedium and restlessness, Thoreau's quiet desperation, in his poem "Peace." He mentored many students, including Herman Wouk, who dedicated his first book to Edman.

> Shall I, I wonder, ever find
> Peace at home in my own mind;
> Or must I to live at all, incur
> Daily the rumor, heat and stir
> That blind the heart and wag the tongue
> Of restless men I move among?
> Is this at every breath the toll
> To twist and fragmentize my soul?
> Must I before I sleep, survey
> Each night the rubbish of each day,
> Meet love in flickering light, hear long
> Dissonances in every song,
> Forsee the sun fade, the dark end
> Shatter the luster of each friend,
> Watch noisy disillusion dart
> Brusque through the quiet of my heart?
> And shall I only when I cease
> To be at all, be all at peace?[13]

The poem is essentially a long question. It begins as one question and throughout poses four additional questions, all rhetorical and all addressed to the narrator of the poem. Will he find any solace or consolation in all of the rubbish that he discards in reviewing each day? The other people in Edman's poem are also restless and find momentary "peace" in rumor and disillusion. We finish the poem and have a disconcerting feeling that our protagonist will not be able to answer the questions he poses, or at least not positively.

In Edman's poem, there is little beneath the surface. The sounds and smells of trains and garbage offer a portrait of a person trapped in one level of existence. We, the readers, are not surprised that the subject of Edman's poem finds no peace, no mental rest from his surroundings. He is not in the countryside, nor is his mind in a place of any repose. He expects little satisfaction and, in that vein, may rightly get all that he anticipates life to offer, which does not amount to much.

Jewish Study as Antidote

One of the cornerstones of Judaism is the centrality of study. We come from a strong intellectual tradition that asks us to probe our world deeply. This daily command and legacy is perhaps the most significant way in which Judaism fights boredom. It asks us to study our universe carefully and engage it with our minds.

In the interpretative community of Judaism, the thousands of years of commentary and scholarship on Jewish texts, Edman's perspective would be debatable. There is an assumption for anyone who reads sacred texts that there is a surface meaning, and there is always something beneath, between the lines. There is a text, a pretext, a subtext, and a context in which everything appears. Even the nature of the printed and sacred Jewish text, surrounded as it is by commentaries, visually communicates that the text never stands alone in isolation. We are always talking about it and around it. The way that Jews have traditionally studied texts is not separate from the way Jews have traditionally lived and made assumptions about life: life is a text that we are constantly interpreting and reinterpreting. An old joke has it that Rashi, perhaps the most famous Jewish commentator on the Bible and Talmud, saw his wife in a new hat and dress and began to share his observations with her on whether he liked the combination. She retorted, "Rashi, can you stop commenting on everything?"

The answer, had one been given, would probably have been "no." We are a commentary people. We engage the world by continually observing, interpreting, and sharing our observations. It is an intellectual tradition that came to envelop an analytical style and, arguably, a way of interacting with the universe. There are exegetes who accepted the fact that not everyone would understand abstraction or that abstraction, as is well known in education, is a developmental stage in intellectual maturation. In other words, surface readings do not always give way to deeper meanings unless we approach the world with certain hermeneutic sensitivities.

Maimonides, in the beginning of *The Guide to the Perplexed* (surely the best title ever given to a book), was certain that his book was not intended for a broad audience and this did not bother him a jot:

> I am the man who when the concern pressed him … and he could find no other device by which to teach a demonstrated truth other than by giving satisfaction to a single virtuous man while displeasing ten thousand ignoramuses—I am he who prefers to address that single man by himself, and I do not heed the blame of those many creatures. For I claim to liberate that virtuous one from that into which he has sunk, and I shall guide him in his perplexity until he becomes perfect and he finds rest.[14]

Maimonides was committed to a narrow audience, one in ten thousand, who could reach perfection through a thorough study of *The Guide* and Judaism's master works and, also, thereby find the consolation of an intellectual friend in a morass of ignorance.

Maimonides also explained that texts are to be understood on multiple levels and that both a wise author and a wise reader would be able to plumb the depths of multivalanced writing that would leave a less able reader in the dark, without even knowing that he was in the dark. "In speaking about very obscure matters it is necessary to conceal some parts and to disclose others."[15]

Maimonides offered a marvelous explanation of what a parable is that illustrates his notion of the multiple layers of interpretation. In commenting on a verse from Proverbs and its Talmudic interpretation, Maimonides developed a theory of reading, suggesting that we get out what we put in when it comes to interpretation:

> The Sage has said: "A word fitly spoken is like apples of gold in filigrees of silver" [Proverbs 25:11].... Hear now an elucidation of the thought that he has set forth. The term *maskiyot* denotes filigree traceries; I mean to say traceries in which there are apertures with very small eyelets like the handiwork of silversmiths. They are so called because a glance penetrates through them.[16]

Maimonides used a biblical verse as a proof text to show that something that looks one way can also look another. He continued to unpack his meaning:

> The Sages accordingly said that a saying uttered with a view to two meanings is like an apple of gold overlaid with silver filigree-work having small holes. How marvelously this describes a well-constructed parable ... in a saying that has two meanings ... the external meaning ought to be as beautiful as silver, while its internal meaning ought to be more beautiful than the external one, the former being in comparison to the latter as gold is to silver.... When looked at from a distance or with imperfect attention, it is deemed to be an apple of silver; but when a keen-sighted observer looks at it with full attention, its interior is clear to him and he knows that it is of gold.[17]

I look at a decorative apple and assume that it is silver. I have not given much thought to the apple as I pass it in a living room or in a natural history museum. And as I speed by I miss the fact that the silverwork contains holes, little apertures, which reveal a rich golden layer beneath. To me, the apple is still outstandingly beautiful, but if someone stopped me and asked, "Did you see the gold apple when you were at so-and-so's house?" I would have to disagree. "No, no. You are mistaken. It was a silver apple. I am sure of it." The questioner would then smile to himself and know that he was one of the ten thousand special and privileged individuals who saw the gold through the silver. Everyone else missed it.

Maimonides also points us to the personal and distinctive nature of reading that we often forget. We sometimes mistakenly think that simply because the same words appear on a page and that letter recognition belongs to every reader that the meaning of the words is also one-dimensional. You see everything that I see when we look at the same letters. Argentinian writer Alberto Manguel, in *A History of Reading*, disabuses us of this notion:

> In every case, it is the reader who reads the sense; it is the reader who grants or recognizes in an object, place or event a certain possible readability; it is the reader who must attribute meaning to a system of signs and then decipher it. We all read ourselves and the world around us in order to glimpse what and where we are. We read to understand, or to begin to understand. We cannot do but read. Reading, almost as much as breathing, is our essential function.[18]

Recognition is the act of the reader alone. To every word read, the reader brings his or her unique universe of understanding: personal history, intellectual range, literary or scientific contexts, mood, emotion, passion, disinterest.

Manguel helps us understand why reading and interpretation are so essential to an approach to boredom. Reading is a primary function. It is the intake or inhalation of a world, whether for recreational, professional, or instructional purposes, much like breathing is to our physical existence. If I am someone for whom the universe is a flat, unmeaningful, neutral landscape on which I conduct my affairs, then I bring that lack of edge and luster to my reading and interpretation of events and possibilities. Contrast that to someone who is filled with enthusiasm and energy, who swallows the universe whole, who interprets events through rose-colored glasses, who makes even the banal aspects of life shine and sparkle.

In Jewish reading terms, we believe not only in surface and deeper meaning. We also subscribe to a more active view of the way that texts talk back.

When Texts Talk Back

What we read also reads us. We engage in conversations with texts because they are speaking to us, in dialogue with us. The *Zohar*, or "Radiant Light," is the central work of the kabbalistic system. In Kabbalah, we venture into another universe of interpretation, where everything in this world and other worlds has meaning beneath, or more appropriately, above the surface. *Kabbalah* means "received" or "tradition" and refers to a body of esoteric Jewish texts credited to medieval thinkers in the scholarly world but dating back to a Sage of the Talmud in traditional religious thinking.

The following parable from the *Zohar* is called "The Old Man and the Ravishing Maiden" (how is that title for combating boredom?) and records an unusual romance:

> Human beings are so confused in their minds. They do not see the way of truth in Torah. She calls out to them every day, in love, but they do not want to turn their heads. She removes a word from her sheath, is seen for a moment, then quickly hides away, but she does so only for those who know her intimately.
>
> A parable. To what can this be compared? To a beloved, ravishing maiden, hidden deep within her palace. She has one lover, unknown to anyone, hidden too. Out of love for her, this lover passes by her gate constantly, lifting his eyes to every side. Knowing that her lover hovers about her gate constantly, what does she do? She opens a little window in her hidden palace, revealing her face to her lover, then swiftly withdraws, concealing

herself. No one near him sees or reflects, only the lover, and his heart and his soul and everything within him flows out to her. He knows that out of love for him she revealed herself for that one moment to awaken love in him.

So it is with a word of Torah: she reveals herself to no one but her lover. Torah knows that one who is wise of heart hovers about her gate every day. What does she do? She reveals her face to him from the palace and beckons him with a hint, then swiftly withdraws to her hiding place.... This is why Torah reveals and conceals herself. With love she approaches her lover to arouse him with love.[19]

The parable unfolds as a reader or student of Torah and the text of the Torah. The two are lovers, which means that love is not one-sided. The reader is not doing all of the work. The text, too, engages the reader, is playful and flirtatious. It reveals itself and then conceals itself and is only apparent to the lover.

How does this work in a textual sense? The writing contains ellipsis and alliterations, repetitions and absent letters. All of these places stop the reader and beg for attention. Thus, commentary comes in to save the day and explain the wordplays and repetitions, unusual word choices and cross-references. If you do not love the text, however, and lavish attention on it, you will not notice any of these hints, these flirtations. You will miss the text speaking to you. Unlike Maimonides' golden apple, which requires the reader's full pause and reflection alone, the ravishing maiden in our parable is working hard to get our attention. She is dancing and singing, opening and closing shutters, beckoning and calling. The love is two-sided. The text, too, is always talking back. It is loving us back, inviting us into its mysteries.

This kabbalistic passage helps us understand that there are solutions to the hermeneutics of boredom not only because we are the readers who interpret life, but also because great texts, like great life opportunities, talk to us and offer us possibilities. When we are bored, we believe that something must entertain us, distract us, or stimulate us. When that fails to happen, we feel that the world has disappointed us;

life has not presented us with opportunities for excitement and growth, wisdom and nurturing. We are entitled to such experiences. But that would be only one way to look at boredom, especially lifestyle boredom.

Another way to view it is through the hermeneutics of boredom. My world is boring because I expect it to be boring, and I fail to do anything about it. After all, my life is a text that I read and reread. I am the reader. I create and sustain meaning. I look for ways to interpret experience. When I am bored, more often than not, I have failed myself. It is not Judaism that is boring; it is the bored way in which I approach my spirituality that is problematic. If I read carefully and with wonder, if I allow texts to flirt with me, then I have successfully cracked open the universe. I am the best reader of my life.

4

Sarcasm, Tedium, and Transgression

> Sarcasm is the language of the devil, for which
> reason I have long since as good as renounced it.
>
> *Thomas Carlyle*

Urban Dictionary, a website of slang definitions offered by random Internet viewers, presents the following definitions of "boredom":

- A severe disease infecting millions of people all over the world in which they constantly exhibit certain behaviors like lack of movement, construction of various pointless structures, doodling, talking about pointless things, and making definitions on UrbanDictionary.com. There is no known cure, though the symptoms do seem to fade when victim is introduced to something time-consuming or slightly entertaining, such as television or counting nails in a wall. Though it is a very severe and widespread epidemic, it is not fatal, though attempts to get rid of the disease have known to be fatal at times. *I made a really long paper clip chain. Want to take pictures of it?*
- Something that makes you do stupid things and then pay for it for the rest of your life.
- What you are probably suffering from if you are reading this definition.

Note that along with the wisecracks that boredom is what stimulated these definitions in the first place, the middle definition explains boredom as a provocateur. It is not simply the absence of excitement, a problem that can be mildly irritating. Stupid acts whose costs can be amortized over a lifetime are boredom's fault. Boredom can be an emotional reaction *to* a situation, an evaluation and review *of* an experience, and an attitude, often characterized by sarcasm and cynicism. Or, as the T-shirt "slogan" says: National Sarcasm Society—Like We Need Your Support.

Sarcasm, while itself not a sin, can lead to transgressive behavior. Disaffection can lead to distraction and, in the worst-case scenario, can spell danger. Milan Kundera, the Franco-Czech novelist, identifies three types of boredom: passive boredom, which he links to disaffected adolescents; active boredom, which he links to kite fliers; and rebellious boredom, which he links to "young people burning cars and smashing shop windows."[1] Violence, self-mutilation, extreme sports, and shoplifting have all been linked with the need to stimulate drama to generate feeling, any feeling. The thrill of taking something that is not yours, hurting someone without consequence, hurting oneself to see blood, all of these have been connected to an escape from the mind-numbing experience of boredom. In other words, boredom can have grave consequences. It is not merely the absence of stimulation; it can lead to overstimulation of a potentially life-threatening variety.

Sarcasm's Sting

The book of Proverbs warns us about the negative influence of sarcasm that can lead to spiritual indifference, resulting in acedia. There, we read, "Cast out the scorner and contention will go out; strife and disgrace will cease" (Proverbs 22:10). Proverbs, part of Judaism's wisdom literature, is filled with advice about becoming smarter, avoiding evil, and being a good neighbor. Wisdom also advises the choice of good company. Our verse tells us the benefits of moving away from scorners; it will clean the air of contention, strife, and disgrace.

What is a scorner? We might call a scorner a critic, a pessimist, a cynic, or a person who uses sarcasm as a way to frame and analyze situations. These individuals ridicule or mock others and, in the process, believe that they elevate themselves. We all recognize the type and its many variations. It is especially prevalent among adolescents. This may be the student who sits at the back of the room, rolling his or her eyes as the teacher speaks. This may be the person who stands at the margins of a crowd who is moved by something but makes fun of it to remain untouched by anything emotional. The effect is disarming; such individuals reek of boredom.

What is the harm of such individuals that Proverbs warns us in such strong terms to cast them out from our social circles? Well, imagine in each of the above scenarios being next to a "scorner." It may affect your own learning and grades in school because, out of a desire to belong, you put on a fake patina of disinterest to seem above your surroundings. It may edge out feelings of beauty and unity in a group setting, and it may give you an upset stomach while eating out. A meal you were enjoying leaves a bad taste in your mouth because someone with more "refined" tastes took the joy out of it. The scorner seems to suck the air out of a room for others. Few scorners keep their feelings to themselves. The pleasure comes in sharing negative observations with others and manipulating the way we view events and encounters so that we begin to see things a cynic's way. What we end up with is a room full of boredom, Jewish institutions brimming with acedia, and a terrible case of indigestion.

Rabbi David Altschuler, a nineteenth-century German rabbi, observes on this verse that when you remove a scorner from your midst, you remove conflict and strife because the cynic often augments arguments by finding fault with people. He comments that this kind of behavior creates more humiliation and prolongs fighting because it assumes a certain attitude about people, one that embodies superiority, suspicion, and derision. Even though we may find a cynic amusing, Proverbs advises us to relinquish sarcasm for friends who embody love and optimism. We will become more loving and hopeful in the process. And we will be less bored, as well.

When Boredom Leads to Violence

No matter the perspective offered on the human role in the world, there is always the worry that without occupation and interest, human beings will naturally gravitate toward transgressive behavior. Literary critic and author Patricia Spacks deals with this issue in her observations on "cultural miasma." Miasma is a menacing or noxious atmosphere that makes boredom sound more dramatic than it appears, "an embracing rubric of discontent," a culture enveloped in anomie. What fills time when there is plenty of time, too much time, to fill?

> Transgression and boredom: the only alternatives. The sphere of transgression enlarges: not just adultery and cocaine, but coffee and chocolate as well. So does that of boredom. We gaze at television to forestall boredom, and television generates more of it.[2]

Just as a reaction to extreme boredom, or "hyperboredom," as Healy puts it,[3] may be alleviated by extreme sports or extreme physical or mental stimulation, so too it may be ameliorated by extreme violence. The lyrics of "Iris," a popular rock song by the Goo Goo Dolls, illustrate this sense of extremity: "You bleed just to know you're alive." Letting blood, an act that is harmful and potentially life-threatening, is used here paradoxically to make us know more alive. Transgressive behavior fills the vacuum created by few alternative modes of stimulation.

The psychologist Erich Fromm discusses the consequences and causes of extreme boredom in his book *The Anatomy of Human Destructiveness*. Fromm does not simply lump together all kinds of boredom but categorizes boredom in terms of human pathology:

> With regard to stimulation and boredom, we can distinguish between [sic] three types of persons: (1) The person who is *capable* of responding productively to activating stimuli is not bored. (2) The person who is in constant need of ever changing, "flat" stimuli is chronically bored, but since he compensates for his boredom, he is not aware of it. (3) The person who fails in the attempt to obtain excitation by any kind of normal stimulation is a very sick individual; sometimes he is acutely aware of his state of mind; sometimes he is not conscious of the fact that he suffers. This type of boredom is fundamentally different from the second type in which boredom is used in a *behavioral* sense, i.e., the person is bored when there is insufficient stimulation,

but he is capable of responding when his boredom is commentated. In the third instance it cannot be compensated.[4]

The one who needs to bleed to feel alive will, according to this categorization, ironically not find relief even when spouting blood. Perhaps boredom will be alleviated momentarily, but the sport of letting blood will soon be like any other stimulation that has lost its appeal. In other words, according to Fromm, for the person who can respond productively to stimuli, boredom will never be a problem. The person who cannot respond even when stimulated will always be bored. This condition Fromm calls depression. In this last category are individuals, according to Fromm, who continuously feel mute and unmoved on any deep level. One who experiences depression, not merely temporary boredom, will anesthetize this "uncomfortable feeling by momentary excitation—'thrill,' 'fun,' liquor, or sex—but *unconsciously* he remains bored."[5] Fromm continues:

> Everybody and everything leaves them cold. They are effectively frozen, feel no joy—but also no sorrow or pain. They feel nothing. The world is gray, the sky is not blue; they have no appetite for life and often would rather be dead than alive.[6]

We have already encountered gray as the color of boredom, and here it is again. The gray in this description is not really gray; it is the way that we can name something that we cannot really name given our human taxonomic limitations: the absence of color. Again, in terms of understanding healthy and unhealthy boredom, Fromm observes that when people complain of depression, they are usually referring to a state of mind; when they say they are bored, they are generally referring to a lack of external stimulation.[7] External stimulation changes more rapidly than a state of mind, which may be a long-term, chronic condition. In healthy boredom, appropriate stimulation will remove the state of boredom:

> The boredom that is overcome by activating stimuli is really ended, or rather it never existed, because the productive person, ideally speaking, is never bored and has no difficulty in finding

the proper stimuli. On the other hand, the unproductive, inwardly passive person remains bored even when his manifest, conscious boredom is relieved for the moment.[8]

Fromm's distinction is important if we are to separate boredom from depression. The inability to relieve boredom is a sign of depression. And yet, in the cultural miasma in which we live, we may find that it is getting harder to find the internal means to manage boredom because we rely so heavily upon external distraction.

Working Your Way Out of Boredom

That boredom could lead to extremism is understood. That boredom can lead to sin and transgressive behavior because of a life without passion is also understandable and is the defining principle behind a Mishnah (a legal teaching that is the foundation for the Talmud):

> The following are the kinds of work that a woman must perform for her husband: grinding corn, baking bread, washing clothes, cooking, nursing her child, making ready his bed, and working in wool. If she brought him one servant, then she need not do any grinding, baking, or washing. Two servants, she need not cook or nurse her child. Three, she need not make his bed or work in wool. Four, and she may lounge in an easy chair. Rabbi Eliezer said, "Even if she brought him a hundred servants, he may compel her to work in wool, since idleness leads to unchasitity." Rabbi Simon ben Gamliel said, "Even if a man forbade his wife under a vow to do any work, he must divorce her and give her a *ketubah* [marriage contract], since idleness leads to idiocy." (Babylonian Talmud, *Ketubot* 59b)

This passage is rich in meaning for a discussion of boredom and affluence. In legal terms, both men and women in the days of the Talmud were required to bring certain economic benefits into the marriage, via dowry, gifts, and/or employment. What if a woman came into marriage with personal wealth and servants? The Mishnah is divided. Some argue that a woman with many attendants need do barely any work other than enjoy her station in life. Others contend that even with all the servants in the world, a woman without work will experience *shi'amum*, "boredom." Boredom may lead to infidelity at worst or to idiocy, foolishness, and thoughtless behavior at the very least.

Rabbi Aaron Lichtenstein, a noted Orthodox rabbi, interprets this passage as a general basis for understanding the emotional import of work:

> In a purely psychological sense, in terms of mental health, one's self-fulfillment comes through work.... The *gemara* [the interpretation of the Mishnah in the Talmud] adds that the more servants she brings, the less she has to do because they will take care of the needs of the household. However, beyond a certain point, this does not apply; her husband can demand that she do something—anything—because, Rabbi Eliezer says, "Idleness leads to lewdness"; it leads to a loose lascivious life.[9]

Work is important because it creates a sense of self-worth and offers a way to fill time that contributes to human productivity.

There is a disagreement within the Mishnah about the consequences of boredom for this woman. Rabbi Lichtenstein attributes Rabbi Simon's strident view to a concern about boredom's potential consequences:

> "*Shi'amum*" can be understood either as insanity or as boredom, ennui, a sense of spiritual degradation. Even if she's as wealthy as Midas, she has to do some kind or work, lest idleness lead to psychological and spiritual problems.[10]

Affluence in this Mishnah contributes to boredom; it does not relieve it. The Mishnah attunes its readers to the dangers of having a staff to do all of the ordinary chores of human living. In the absence of productivity and structure, the human mind will entertain transgression. The formula, as articulated in the Mishnah, is unambiguous. Do something meaningful or you will do something that courts danger.

Keeping Too Busy

When boredom mixes with a negative view of the world, it produces a cocktail that can have long-term consequences. Film critic and author David Denby, in a *New Yorker* article called "Buried Alive: Our Children and the Avalanche of Crud," states:

> The danger is not mere exposure to occasional violent or prurient images but the acceptance of a degraded environment that devalues everything—a shadow world in which our kids are breathing in a lot of poison without knowing that there's clean air and sunshine elsewhere. They are shaped by the media as consumers before they've had a chance to develop their souls.[11]

The arrested development of these young souls is due to an obscuring of values and meaning, which are more arduous to achieve and personally more demanding of us than entertainment. We seek relief where it cannot be found and can busy ourselves into thinking that the solution lies in greater distraction, when the solution to boredom really lies in a search for greater purpose.

Human beings are addicted to meaning. We all have a great problem, which, in reality, is a great strength. Our lives must have some sort of content, as we concluded in chapter 1. We cannot bear to live our lives without some sort of substance that we can see as constituting meaning. Meaninglessness is boring. And boredom can be described metaphorically as a meaning withdrawal. "In order to remove this discomfort, we attack the symptoms rather than the disease itself and search for all sorts of meaning-surrogates."[12]

Boredom and Choice

Shopping is a big meaning-surrogate in our culture. It, too, is a symptom or expression of larger social ennui. When we buy a computer, spend a Sunday afternoon shopping as a hobby, or perseverate for hours on buying an item to our exact specifications online, we generate more choices so that we distract ourselves from boredom with lots of options and remarkable personalization. We go to the supermarket and confront eighty different brands of shampoo, forty types of coffee, brand after brand of cereal. Shopping takes longer and becomes much more customized; the smallest consumer purchase can begin us on a quest for inner identity. Is this me?

When we have too many choices, does boredom go or does it grow? Professor and author Barry Schwartz, in *The Paradox of Choice*, believes that too much choice can prevent us from making wise choices, can generate too many unsatisfied expectations, and can even paralyze us from making any decisions at all.[13]

If we keep choosing and keep shopping, then we will always embrace newness and minimize boredom. When that newness fades or wears off, we can make another job change or move house or handle a problem with a little retail therapy. But such approaches themselves can become tedious and not really provide the excitement anticipated after a while. Even road warriors get tired.

From a spiritual perspective, Judaism and Jewish institutions are taking quite a blow from the changes in our styles of decision making. Judaism is not a brand of coffee, but it is a choice for today's Jews rather than an obligation. Making decisions about where to locate yourself as a Jew today is starting to look a lot more like being in a grocery store than being in a synagogue. If you can have your computer and iPod customized to your very specific tastes, then religion should fit that way, too. Relaxed fit or tailored. The highly nuanced insider language of personal choices reveals community affiliations in the slight differences of yarmulke styles or skirt lengths. Synagogues and Jewish institutions, too, are bending in lots of ways to the power of these market forces, trying hard to outreach to people with different kinds of programs and faces.

It is commitment, not having choices, that provides the real relief to boredom, because it helps us develop stronger personal identities. The very act of committing ourselves to our choices can create a sense of joy and completion. The Rabbinic expression *"Ain simkha k'hatarot ha-sfakot,"* "There is no happiness like the resolution of doubt," speaks powerfully to the way that commitment helps resolve deep-seated ambiguities about ourselves and the world. Rabbi David Altschuler, whom we encountered earlier, uses this very expression in his explication of Proverbs 15:30, "What brightens the eye, gladdens the heart...." While other commentators read the brightening of the eye as an aesthetic or intellectual response, Rabbi Altschuler understands it as the resolution of doubt. Commitment does not only mean that we are losing an ability to choose. It may also mean we are gaining a deeper understanding of ourselves, our values, and our needs in the process. This process of self-definition brightens the eye and gladdens the heart. There is almost a sense of exuberance in this reading; we are capable of minimizing boredom because of personal growth and the ability to solve problems. We love puzzles and mind games, especially when we are at their center.

From One Extreme to the Other

If we could, in the realm of religion, find an adequate antonym to "boring," it would be "passionate." We are all moved by passion. We can tell when an employee is passionate about work, a volunteer is passionate about a cause, and a graduate student is passionate about a subject. While we can find passion objectionable and intolerant, we generally find passion in these endeavors to be refreshing. In a time of lukewarm emotion, we welcome emotions that are expressed strongly with intensity, enthusiasm, and ardor. But the boundary lines between exuberance and intolerance are getting harder to negotiate within religion. The lion's self-restraint we mentioned earlier would perhaps serve the institutional religious world well right now, when too much passion has led to bloodshed and a disgrace of religion in the eyes of secular nonbelievers. There is room for passionate moderation that has not yet been well articulated.

One way that religion has combated the spiritual boredom that can result in violence is to enhance religious passion or zealotry. And yet, on the surface, this rise in passion may be causing more of a problem for religion than is desirable. One of the great worries of our age is religious fundamentalism. Its emergence as a force of world violence today is not all that surprising. Perceptions about religion generally and Judaism specifically are that it is tepid, distilled of content and wonder, stale, and unresponsive to modernity.

There appear to be two prevalent responses to lukewarm Judaism. Adamant believers try to vivify it by embracing it with raw emotion, what we call fundamentalism. Alternatively, modern Judaism has become a casualty of postmodern eclecticism and privatization. Many believe that all expressions of Judaism are equally valid, making religion so neutral that it has little impact. Religious fundamentalism can be loud, public, unambiguous, and exciting. Private religion hardly makes any noise and can be so self-determined that it sacrifices rigor, history, and discipline.

When we speak of boredom that can lead to violence, we have to bear in mind the impact of religious fundamentalism on tolerance and understand that if we do little to make religion interesting, some people will relieve their spiritual boredom by throwing stones. Or worse.

Nothing to Do
5 in the Village
Boredom in Community

There's little left but to be bored or bore.

Lord Byron

What happens when the something that's boring you really isn't you, it's someone else? Marriages can get boring. We can grow out of friendships. We can even tire of an entire community of people when there is insufficient diversity. Living in community can be a wonderful bonding and nurturing experience. We feel cared for and loved and helped when we live in intimate association with others. It can also be remarkably predictable and dull. At each event, we tend to see the same people, who move with us in the same ways, often at the same location. We come to be overfamiliar with communal habits, the behaviors and rituals that stretch across individuals and impact us as a group.

When we close our eyes, we might see a highly choreographed dance in a synagogue sanctuary: "Please rise. Please be seated. Recite together." We know this dance so well that it fails to engage us. Think of a long string of bar or bat mitzvah ceremonies where we watch one nervous child after another read a speech or a haftarah; the rabbi congratulates the child warmly and kvells at the family. The mother takes out a hankie, dabs her eyes, then shuffles everyone into the social hall for the same frosted brownies at the *kiddush* (special blessing) that are served every week. Sometimes there is a dramatic change. The brownies have walnuts.

We Are All Individuals

After a while, these well-oiled, well-orchestrated events blend into one, and we stop paying attention to the dance moves of communal rituals because we can do them in our collective sleep. Sometimes the only bright spark in the anticipated movements is when the bar mitzvah is not someone else's but our own. But do we really have to suffer through so many until the dance belongs to us?

According to philosopher Sebastian de Grazia, communities can contain the boredom of individuals because we have become so institutionalized that it is hard to tell a bored person in a community from one who is not bored:

> Small communities do contain bored persons. The community's adaptation to them proceeds gradually, later becoming institutionalized so that the bored are hard to find from the outside looking in.[1]

It is not hard to fake belonging because it is often a matter of knowing the moves or the right dress or the insider language that separates your group. Recently, I was at a wedding party where the groom addressed his parents' community in the following way: "You know, when I was a kid I thought that this was the most boring community, but now that I am married I have come to appreciate it as a great place to bring up a family." What were we supposed to think? Someone has just told me that I am dull, but it's okay because boredom has its long-term rewards. The suburbs may not be exciting, but they produce nice, well-adjusted children. As for the parents, just grin, bear it, and discuss lawnmowers.

Before we venture on a full-blown discussion of boredom within faith communities, it's important to establish a consensus around what *community* means. *Community* is not a simple entity or organism. Technically, a community may be any group of more than one; generally, we regard communities as interconnected groupings consisting of many. Individuals living or acting in community may be brought together by virtue of geography, ideology, shared values, interests, or shared institutions. We tend to view our local communities in this very way. I may use the term *community* with regard to the people who live within a few blocks of my home or the cluster of individuals involved with my children's education. I may use it to refer to the staff at my workplace if I feel particularly linked to them as friends or because they are similarly enmeshed in the same mission. I may use it to describe the congregants in my local synagogue or a group of friends who have been getting together the third Thursday of every month to study together. Perhaps my community is the members of my book club or those in my stamp-collecting orbit. Community can encompass and overlap with all of these groups, even if they have little or no relation to each other.

The Jewish community broadly shares each one of the characteristics mentioned above. Often Jewish communities are geographically linked and also joined by shared values and ideology. But we also use the term *Jewish community* to refer to an intangible entity of compassion and caring. The Jewish community may be a global network of people who take care of each other even if they have not met, like a large, extended family who rarely, if ever, get together but who will be there for each other in times of crisis. Many Jewish charities rely upon this very broad sense of community when doing their fundraising and offering their assistance. Sometimes, these intangible webs can ironically carry more meaning for people than real communities. Such imagined communities, to borrow a sociological term,[2] can be even more compelling because we do not see their inside workings; we only feel ourselves to be part of them. This feeling can be psychically very powerful. It is also hard to get bored of a community that you cannot see or experience.

As we can see, ideas about community are so broad, so expansive in their capacity to hold people, that the very notion of community has been questioned altogether. Some philosophers believe that there is no firm consensus of meaning or definition for *community*; anything you say about *community* in defining it can be contested.[3] There are philosophers who say that *community* is a word we use to mask the inherent inequalities or fissures in any given grouping.

Some argue that communities have to be face to face, whilst others allow that they may unite those who do not know each other.... Some argue that communities must involve relationships of a certain moral quality, whilst others allow that feelings of solidarity may be sufficient, even if these feelings rest upon illusions or misconceptions about the moral character of the relationship. These disputes, coupled with the sheer variety of its ordinary and theoretical uses, can give rise to the worry that "community" is employed by people simply to commend the social arrangements they happen to favor.[4]

We call something a community to make us feel better about belonging when, in actuality, there are many divisions within the group. Be that as it may, communities that are joined together by shared behaviors or shared space can, and arguably must, also be joined together by shared boredom. Why?

Homophily: Not That There's Anything Wrong with That

We tend to associate, seek out, or enjoy the company of those most like us for friendships, partnerships, and marriage. *Homophily* is the name that sociologists give to the relationship of people who are attracted to those similar to themselves.[5] They may hold the same beliefs, be they political or religious, or share a similar education, age, gender, or economic status. I sit in the carpool lane, wondering why everyone seems to have the same Honda Odyssey as I do in the same color (a bluish silver). But it shouldn't really surprise me because in a world where we have so much choice, how do we know we've made the right choices, whether it's the purchase of a car or the choice of political party? Probably the most significant way we affirm our choices is by aligning ourselves with others who make the same choices we make.

Sociologists distinguish between status homophily and value homophily. In status homophily, people are attracted to each other by virtue of a shared position within a hierarchy, be it financial or other. For example, friendships may develop between two people who go to the same country club and discover that both of their children also go to the same prep school. Value homophily brings people together not by external measurements of success or station but by virtue of shared ideas or values. The two people in the country club almost become fast friends until one realizes that the other loves to big-game hunt. Now they don't speak to each other.

Within many communities, people associate with those with whom there is both status homophily *and* values homophily. These double bonds can be particularly tight. Two board members of a synagogue both live in the same neighborhood, keep kosher, and find that they both appear on the same plaque announcing their gift to the synagogue's capital campaign. By "chance" they discover that they both had the same brownies at their sons' *b'nei mitzvah*. With walnuts.

"By chance" is an interesting turn of phrase. Many people within tight-knit communities are astounded by the amount of serendipity in their lives when, in actuality, the chances of *not* making these connections is probably more remarkable. When we gravitate toward people who are like us, we naturally find many different ways in which our lives replicate each others, albeit with slight variations. Consequently, we may have children of similar ages, take vacations in similar locations, and vote the same way. There are few surprises on that front. The "chance" similarities are often nothing more than positive confirmations that we have made the "right" choices because others also shop in the same stores or support similar charities. In such settings, the primal fear we experience is not being like everyone else and a victim of convention but precisely the opposite. We profoundly fear being alone, acting independently, setting ourselves apart.

Boredom, if it keeps us in community and sustains belonging, is admissible and acceptable, because we tell ourselves that it is a small price to pay to keep us in a community of like-minded individuals who share and confirm our deeply held values. It may be a comfort; it is not always honest.

This social contract may be true for some people living in community, but it is not true for everyone. The former may make the unfortunate error of assuming that the way they experience and enjoy community is universally felt. They willingly accept the boredom they experience around communal rites and behaviors because the benefits, in their minds, far outweigh the tedium: they do not want to feel isolated. In every community, however, there are individuals who are there via attachment to someone else, a spouse or child, parent or best friend, who suffer boredom silently for the sake of love, responsibility, or obligation to others:

> "I don't believe in God, but I go to synagogue for my kids because I think it's important that they get raised in this lifestyle. You know, the family that prays together stays together."

> "We eat Friday night dinners as a family mostly because my elderly mother insists on it, and you don't want to cross her. It's just easier to show up than to make excuses."

> "I hate Hebrew school, but my mom forces me to go. I may have to be there, but I don't have to like it."

> "I joined the board of the JCC because it was really important to my husband, who has been a member all his life. It's not meaningful to me, but he is so proud of me that I can't break it to him that I can't stand going to the meetings. I just make grocery lists and watch the clock."

Living the Paradox

In each of these cases, these individuals harbor the secret or not-so-secret knowledge that life does not have to be this way but there are things we do to keep other people happy that involve our own sacrifice of excitement.

The things we do for someone else that provide us with little pleasure and may even bore us to tears are not simple sacrifices, nor do they always achieve the ends that we generously were willing to undertake for a positive outcome. Parents who suffer stale rituals and services for "the sake of the children" are usually passing down only one value: Judaism bores me, and it will bore you, too. A lifeless religious tradition passed down only for the sake of passing it down will neither engage nor sustain interest. We become fake role models of something we may believe in principle but not deeply care about in practice. Our body language betrays us. Children are highly attuned to picking up insincerity. If you have accepted a boring Jewish lifestyle for the sake of your children, your spouse, your parents, or your social associations, think again. Most people can see through us. We may unwittingly communicate daily through personal religious lethargy that boredom is a sufficient and acceptable price to pay to live within community to those who may not see the value of such a spiritual wager.

We may make such mental contracts because we do not believe that we have a choice otherwise. Again de Grazia observes:

> To be a bored person you must believe, I think, that something both interesting to do and permissible exists somewhere. Either he hasn't the external means or is prevented by morality or hasn't the knowledge of what to do but believes that the knowledge exists somewhere.[6]

Our failure of imagination, our acceptance that someone else is having a better time elsewhere, however, is not a cost that all are willing to pay. There are thinkers who believe that many of the most interesting people are not willing to compromise on personal satisfaction for the sake of community.[7]

We live with a strange paradox. We want to be around people who are like us, while at the same time, we crave the new and different. We use the same clichés to mark events and situations. *Mazel tov. He should grow up to be healthy. She looks just like her mother. And then there are other occasions. It's just tragic. She was so young. There are no words. It's the circle of life. They make a lovely couple. No really.* And yet we may feel, even while we are emitting the words, that they lack all originality. I remember sharing the expense of a gift and the writing of a card with someone on the occasion of a mutual friend's wedding. When I questioned whether what she wrote might have sounded a tad cliché, she responded, "But it's different because I *really* mean it."

Don't Step on My Four Cubits

Finding a way to express individuality within community can be an immense challenge. The English businessman and journalist Walter Bagehot (1826–87), almost two hundred years ago, observed that community can squelch individuality:

> What espionage of despotism comes to your door so effectually as the eye of the man who lives at your door? Public opinion is a permeating influence, and it exacts obedience to itself; it requires us to think other men's thoughts, to speak other men's words, to follow other men's habits.[8]

We don't want to be creatures of someone else's habits. We want to express ourselves. We deeply believe that self-expression is not boring and that living with others may be dull or limit our independence. In a cartoon from *The Far Side* collection, a sheep stands on his hind legs amidst the cluster of cotton tufts of his companions, throws up his front legs in alarm, and says, "Wait! Wait! Listen to me! ... We don't HAVE to just be sheep," with a look of great relief and delight.[9]

Proverbs, once again, offers us some advice to avoid the pitfalls of communal living that can lead to overfamiliarity and a compromise of our individuality: "Withdraw your foot from your neighbor's house, lest he become tired of you and then hate you" (Proverbs 25:17). Give space to your neighbors so that they will not tire of your constant presence and come to detest you, or at least find you mildly irritating. This demand to provide comfortable boundaries is one of several ways that Judaism tries to manage the boredom that is a natural outgrowth of living in close proximity to others.

In Rabbinic law, there is a literal and metaphoric boundary that helps protect us against the incursion of others, an amount of space that each person occupies in this world and in our eternal resting place: four cubits. Four cubits is a measurement that approximates about six feet. In Jewish law, your burial space is four cubits around. In prayer, you have four cubits of white space in which to pray where no one can obstruct you.[10] No one should go before you or behind you in an intrusive way while you are praying the central standing prayer, the *Amidah*. If you are excommunicated for any reason, others are not allowed near you, *near* being defined as four cubits away. The minimum size that a space can be to be called a human habitation is four cubits, and anyone within four cubits of an elderly person must stand in respect. If you are within four cubits of a king or person of particular wisdom, you must make a blessing on that individual's authority or scholarship. An old person is old within his four cubits, and a scholar is wise within his. Encroaching upon this personal space cannot be done without permission or notice of some kind.

Even God has only four cubits of space in this world, as is recorded in the Babylonian Talmud, which states that since the destruction of the Temple, God has only four cubits of Jewish law alone (*Berakhot* 8a). The text is trying to communicate that where God's presence was once experienced broadly through Temple service and sacrifice, it is now relegated only to the interaction that God has with those who study Judaism with intensity and make a place for God in a Temple-less universe. If God has the personal space relegated to human beings, then it is clear that human beings must give each other this space when interacting.

The Importance of Individuation

More than offer some white space of a predetermined nature alone, Jewish law is trying to help us establish theoretical guidelines for living well and creatively within community so that we can find room for individuality while still benefiting from and enjoying the company of others. This recognition of the self apart and distinct from others is a key to being human, maturing, and avoiding the inevitable tedium that comes with communal living. According to Erich Fromm, in *The Sane Society*, a person reaches a critical place in his own growth where he must define a concept of self; without it a person would question his sanity: "Only after he has conceived of the outer world as separate and different from himself does he come to the awareness of himself as a distinct being, and one of the last words he learns to use is 'I' in reference to himself."[11]

It is hard to find this "I" in a world where "we" is more common. Fromm continues, "In the development of the *human race* the degree to which man is aware of himself as a separate self depends on the extent to which he has emerged from the clan and the extent to which the process of individuation has developed."[12] Living in too close proximity to others can inhibit the process of individuation where I begin to see myself as separate from the family and community that surrounds me. We need to develop our own four cubits of personal space, even when others are not anxious to offer it.

One of the most famous Hasidic statements about the importance of individuality and how easy it is to lose it in community is that of the Kotzker Rebbe, a staunch individualist:

> If I am I because I am I, and you are you because you are you, then I am I and you are you. However, if I am I because you are you, and you are you because I am I, then I am not I and you are not you.[13]

I cannot be myself if that being is only determined by others. My ability to be myself will depend largely on my intellectual interests, emotional inner life, creativity, confidence, and sense of uniqueness. It is these qualities that will help me separate from others and find my distinctiveness. Our own boredom can reflect an angst about the insufficiently individuated self.[14]

Inviting the Other

If we are interested in the four-cubit approach to maintaining a healthy balance of self and other to keep boredom in check, how can we be sure that others will really respect our cubits and keep them truly people-free? Abraham Joshua Heschel writes about the behaviors of Hasidic master Rabbi Nachman of Breslov's students. The famous rabbi called upon his disciples to meditate in solitude for at least an hour every day, in a room or outdoors. Heschel writes, "I recall that in the prayer rooms of his followers in Warsaw, there were narrow cells in which individuals could retire for an hour or more, since their homes were overcrowded and the surrounding fields offered no seclusion."[15] Yeshiva education included an unusual feature, time alone to confront the self in a genuine way.[16]

Perhaps Rabbi Nachman understood that he had to help his disciples experience individuation in a distinctive and authentic way. Nothing teaches us more about managing boredom than enforced time alone without distraction. This time ironically means that when others do enter our lives, we recognize them with more consciousness, even celebration.

On a more profound level, the invitation to the other is a recognition of the needs, wants, and desires of another human being. This also implies that an invitation to someone else is not only about rights and wants but also about responsibility. Living in community makes us aware that we are responsible for redeeming the lives of others to the extent that we can. In the words of Rabbi Joseph Soloveitchik, one of the towering Talmudists and philosophers of the twentieth century:

> Once I have recognized the thou and invited him to join the community, I ipso facto assume responsibility for the thou. Recognition is identical with commitment.... I assume responsibility for each member of the community to whom I have granted recognition and whom I have found worthy of being my companion. In other words, the I is responsible for the physical and mental welfare of the thou.[17]

For Rabbi Soloveitchik, the recognition of otherness implies commitment. The moment I recognize the existence of someone else, I take responsibility for that person on some level. Rabbi Soloveitchik finds that this interaction is best expressed in the act of collective prayer; a congregation at worship typifies, for him, a united I-Thou relationship:

> When the I becomes aware of his being responsible for the well-being of the thou, whom he has helped bring into existence, a new community emerges: the community of prayer. What does this mean? It means a community of common pain, of common suffering.[18]

Shared pain is an act in community that tends to be genuinely interesting. People have often described the experience of being prayed for by a group as powerfully supportive in a time of crisis. The group tears at a funeral and the loving web of connections manifest at a house of mourning during shiva often create this tender, prayerful sense of community that usually lacks tedium. Why? We can possibly explain this by virtue of the fact that sadness and tragedy are always less boring than emotional neutrality or even happiness. It is pain, and not pleasure, that ironically generates originality and introspection. Again, we can count on good old King Solomon for his Ecclesiastical wisdom: "It is better to go to a house of mourning than a house of celebration" (Ecclesiastes 7:2).

When we pray with intentionality for someone else or mourn the loss of someone, we are entering the world of their individuation. What makes a truly great funeral distinctive from a mediocre or run-of-the-mill funeral is the speaker's ability to capture the uniqueness of the loved one, the distinctive qualities that make that person *worth* mourning, that make the loss so gaping, that create the hole in the universe that cannot be filled. At a truly great funeral we might oddly find a new and unfamiliar person emerging in our imaginations. Boring funerals are those in which no original word is uttered and the eulogy could describe the person in the casket in front of us and about a thousand of our closest friends and acquaintances. *He was truly kind. A very giving person. She was a wonderful mother. She will be missed by all.* When we create a personal identity of the dead that is full of clichés, then we have not created the person who we and others will really miss because he or she is just like everyone else. Death should never be boring. That which torments us offers us meaning.

Sadly, communities often escape the boredom of suburban sameness of split-levels and vanilla social events because there is usually enough tragedy to keep us powerfully involved with others. Mental anguish has its side benefits. It helps us feel alive, appreciative of our own good fortunate, or able to appreciate the kindness of others toward us; it shakes the leadenness off. One good funeral and we might realize why we live where we do or why we work where we do or why, indeed, we wake up each morning.

Self and Social Capital

We do not live only or primarily in community to feel pain together. We live with each other to celebrate each other's successes and because social pressure helps us do good within our communities, even if we may lack the do-gooder impulses ourselves. Our social contract is a function of choices. Sociologists have a name for this reciprocity: social capital. This is, roughly speaking, the investment we make in other people and institutions that help locate us advantageously in an interconnected social construct. For example, I may buy two tickets to my synagogue dinner honoring a couple who were stalwart figures in the synagogue's last capital campaign. The wife in this couple is also a partner in a law firm that I work in, and I would like to be a partner in myself. Social capital, this web of connections, as opposed to human capital (individual talents, education, and personal initiative), is arguably more helpful in placing people in situationally positive and helpful positions in society.

Many communities are so tightly woven that "unintended" social, economic, educational, and spiritual benefits accrue to their members as a result of their community connections. But you must pay to play. You pay in dues, literal or figurative. You cannot expect to keep attending a local community center if you are not technically a member. You cannot expect someone to be there to provide comfort at your time of loss if you never attend the shiva houses of others. Significant studies in the past decades have demonstrated the gradual breakdown of social capital precisely because we live in units where every individual believes that individual rights are more important than collective pressures to conform. With that loss, the advantages of social capital are obviously minimized. Professor and author Robert Putnam, in *Bowling Alone*, writes:

> If we lack that social capital, economic sociologists have shown, our economic prospects are seriously reduced, even if we have lots of talent and training. Similarly, communities that lack civic interconnections find it harder to share information and thus mobilize to achieve opportunities or resist threats.[19]

In a time of individual rights where social capital is not valued, we begin to lose our footing, even our economic grounding. We become harder to mobilize collectively for the good. It takes more efforts to resist threat. There are dangers lurking for those who minimize social capital, dangers that have yet to be fully understood. Social capital can only be acknowledged and nurtured where there is a willingness to sign a social contract that limits individual freedoms to gain other kinds of benefits. The investments made to create social capital may not always be exciting; they may be downright boring, but it beats the alternative.

This bargain or deal we make has been called a capital improvement in the world of sociology. Capital improvement is beneficial to us as individuals because it is responsible for

> widening our awareness of the many ways in which our fates are linked. People who have active and trusting connections to others—whether family members, friends, or fellow bowlers—develop or maintain character traits that are good for the rest of society. Joiners become more tolerant, less cynical, and more empathetic to the misfortunes of others. When people lack connections to others, they are unable to test the veracity of their own views, whether in the give-and-take of casual conversations or in more formal deliberation. Without such an opportunity, people are more likely to be swayed by their worst impulses.[20]

On a spiritual level, even when communal living is not exciting, it is a safeguard to protect us against our worst selves. It creates mechanisms for compassion and sustains our values across generations and important milestones. To benefit from its advantages, we need both to sustain and support others and to protect ourselves.

All of this reasoning can be self-serving. Within Jewish terms, virtually all of Jewish law involving human interactions is not about social capital but kindness capital. We help others because of the power of giving. We make deposits of *hesed*, lovingkindness, not to protect our selfish interests but in order to get beyond the self. We find meaning and purpose in our own living when we stop living only for ourselves. In the words of the psalmist, "The world is built on kindness" (Psalm 89:3).

Buber offers us a good formula for living within community while protecting the personal space and uniqueness that can quell boredom: "To begin with oneself but not to end with oneself. To start with oneself but not to aim at oneself. To comprehend oneself but not be preoccupied with oneself."[21] To minimize boredom in community, we have to tend to our four cubits and then move far beyond them to reach out with grace and compassion to others.

6

Prayer, Habituation, and Holy Insecurity

There is a vast difference between saying prayers and praying.

Morris Joseph

The next time you are in front of a computer with a few minutes on your hands, punch in "Mr. Bean in Church" on your search engine. Ten minutes later you will have viewed what is perhaps the best comic routine on boredom in prayer. Mr. Bean, played by the English comedian Rowan Atkinson, is a nervous congregant who comes into a service late. He sits in the front pew, forgetting a hymnal, sharing one with a fellow congregant but out of step with the others, singing off-key, barely aware of the correct words. The congregation then sits, and poor Mr. Bean suffers the sermon. He holds in a sneeze until it explodes fabulously all over himself. Then, trying to fake attentiveness, he begins to drift off into a powerful sleep, falling onto the shoulder of his neighbor, finally dropping all the way to the floor in full splay. Suddenly, he wakes up, shakes his sleep, and sits back down, holding his eyelids wide open so that he dare not nap again. Fighting boredom with food, he wrestles a candy wrapper, the noisy cellophane kind that attracts too much attention, until it too falls to the floor, and in a religious sign of the cross that he sweeps across his chest for distraction, he visits the floor again, trying to retrieve the candy that he lost, the saving grace of his morning, the only thing that will keep him awake until the service ends.

We recognize the signs of cathedral doldrums all too well in our own sanctuaries. Boredom is the hallmark of the tired synagogue service, collapsing under the weight of habituation. A student once confessed to me that she found walks to be a more spiritual alternative to synagogue services because "at least when you walk, you are doing something." The implication of this should make any of us shudder. Does a synagogue service require nothing, accomplish nothing? Obviously, this woman is not the only one struggling with shul blues; Jewish historian Jack Wertheimer, in the *American Jewish Year Book 2005*, titles an article "The American Synagogue: A House of Boredom, Worship, or What?"[1] The boldness of the question is striking.

This malaise does not only affect those in the pews; sometimes it even describes those on the *bimah* (the synagogue's front platform from which the rabbi and cantor lead the service). A contemporary rabbi confessed that during his childhood, he hid novels in the crease of his prayer book. He thought no one was looking until the rabbi, escorting the Torah through the sanctuary, caught him red-handed: "See me at the *kiddush* after services." After an excruciatingly long service made worse by the rabbi's threatening demand, the young man found the rabbi during the *kiddush*, and the rabbi asked him directly, "Are you bored in services?"

> I paused. Did he really ask me if I was bored? Was he living on another planet? Everyone is bored in services. I wanted to laugh out loud. However, I did not want to get grounded by my parents so I hesitated, "Do you really want the truth?" He looked me straight in the eye. I whispered, "Well, rabbi, yes." Suddenly his face was right in front of mine. I thought, "I'm in big trouble now." But then he whispered back: "So am I." I could not believe my ears. The great and awesome rabbi just told me that he is bored in services. Before I could digest that, he asked, "So what are you going to do about it?" I think I have been trying to answer this question ever since.[2]

For decades this rabbi struggled with the question his childhood rabbi put to him in an awkward set of circumstances. He did not have an easy answer, yet he engaged profoundly with the question. What should we do about boredom in the synagogue and in prayer? The two are not the same.

Many traditional Jews wake up, brush their teeth, pray, eat breakfast, and go on with their religious routines with little expectation of prayer's purposefulness or even disappointment when prayer does not deliver any spiritual jolt. When prayer becomes the spiritual equivalent of brushing our teeth, we worry. We should worry.

How Do You Solve a Problem like *Tefilah*?

Prayer (*tefilah*), an act that without intention amounts to air, is one of the hardest of Jewish habits to keep fresh and vibrant when practiced regularly. Prayer in a synagogue can be even harder because the institutional structure, the distraction of big hats and unmatched socks, friends a few seats away and large-scale community events like basketball-themed *b'nei mitzvah*, all seem to get in the way of a conversation with God. One poster in a synagogue I spotted in a northwest London synagogue unabashedly put the issue to its members this way: "If you come here to talk, where do you go to *daven* (the Yiddish word for *pray*)?"

A basic legal requirement of Jewish prayer is understanding the simple meaning of the words in the *siddur*, or Jewish prayer book, in Hebrew, the *perush ha-milim*. But words without feelings in prayer are empty. Hannah, who is the great model of prayer in the Rabbinic tradition, prayed with such emotion that Eli, the reigning high priest at the time, accused her of drunkenness. She corrected him: "I have been pouring out my heart to the Lord" (1 Samuel 1:14–15).

Within Hasidic traditions of prayer, supplicants achieve greater *kavanna* (intentionality) by going beyond the plain meaning of the language. Chief among the Hasidic techniques recommended to attenuate *kavanna* is the mantra, repeated word or words from the prayer book or a name of God that helps strengthen focus. As in many forms of meditation, the objective is to transcend the word through deep concentration on the actual letters so that other distractions fall to the wayside.

Alternatively, reading prayer by moving from letter to letter and unifying the letters into words becomes a symbolic act of unifying disparate entities to achieve wholeness and harmony. In the words of one Hasidic master:

> When he prays, a man should put all his strength into the utterances … he should proceed from letter to letter until he has forgotten his corporeal nature. He should reflect on the idea that the letters become combined and joined one to the other and this is a great delight. For if in the material world unification is attended by delight how much more so in the spiritual realms![3]

Intentionality in prayer is so desired that Simhah Bunem of Pzhysha, a Hasidic rabbi, used to complain of headaches during prayer—his concentration was that strong. He sought the advice of a master who told him that he was praying with his head more than his heart. After he heard this, he claimed that he never suffered from headaches again.[4] Being present in an act of prayer is one way to eliminate boredom, although sustaining such high levels of concentration can be difficult. If you're praying from the wrong part of yourself, your brain may even start to hurt.

Another prominent technique within Hasidut is the movement of the body during prayer. This is another means to take prayer out of the cognitive arena and make it physical and experiential, minimizing tedium by making prayer active. Hasidim are known for gesturing wildly during prayer, sometimes beginning their prayers on one side of the room and finding themselves on the other by their conclusion. Swaying and bowing during prayer is older than the Hasidic movement, however; the Bible records instances of kneeling, spreading the hands toward heaven, and prostration.[5] Psalms offers a rationale for movement during prayer: "All my bones shall say, 'Lord, who is like You?'" (Psalm 35:10). It is not only the mind or heart that is activated during intense prayer; the body itself becomes animated. Movement can help prayer become less static and more resonant.

Preparing for Prayer: More Practical Tips

Minimizing boredom in prayer is largely a matter of proper preparation. In a famous responsum of the sixteenth century, *halakhic* authority Rabbi David ibn Zimra writes of the importance of praying only when you are serene and in a good temper. He also recommends that you pray in a place where you are socially accepted and not in contention with others and where your heart desires to be with people who can inspire. He even recommends gazing or imagining a person you respect to help you achieve better focus: "When a man looks at his friend or his relative or his teacher or one who pleases him, his soul is awakened to an elevated degree of concentration and an additional spirit on high rests upon him."[6]

Think of a role model when you pray. We watch people to improve our skills all the time, from athletes to cooking shows on television. And yet, how many of us can say that we have a mentor in prayer, a personal trainer to achieve spiritual goals?

Maimonides, a medieval philosopher and physician, advises that certain practical acts of preparation take place before praying to enhance the experience. They work well both within and outside of the synagogue experience.[7] Maimonides, in "Laws of Prayer," combs through the Talmud and recommends the following behaviors:

- Using proper posture and positioning.
- Facing the direction of the ancient Temple once housed in Jerusalem before its destruction.
- Physically preparing the body before prayer, like relieving yourself, to avoid physical distraction.
- Fixing your clothing so that you look fit to pray and feel unencumbered.
- Situating yourself with a place to pray so that ideally you return to the same place and create a sacred space for yourself. This may inspire quiet meditation and offer some psychic if not a real modicum of privacy. Maimonides also advises removing any bad-smelling material and distancing yourself from malodorous distractions.

- Preparing your voice so that you can enunciate words properly without, at the same time, being a disturbance to a neighbor.
- Readying yourself for bowing, a physical accompaniment and gesture of humility during prayer. While we may have limited physical gestures in today's modern service, those that we do have should be done, according to Maimonides, with thoughtfulness and preparation.[8]

Translating these into modern prayer behaviors is not difficult. We understand that we have to minimize distraction for any meaningful encounter and maximize our ability to appreciate wonder, to create harmony with God, and to be in consonance with our surroundings. Each of Maimonides' suggestions also involves different senses because smells, sounds, and sights can either help enhance wonder or inhibit it completely. There is a centeredness that Maimonides emphasizes in this passage that sensitizes us to the role of place and location in prayer. Pick the wrong seat and you've practically kissed a good prayer opportunity goodbye. Seating yourself next to the shul yenta or the friend who has not made personal hygiene a priority was probably a mistake.

Once More with Feeling: Boredom and Habituation

Practical recommendations to enhance prayer can make you more present in the moment of prayer; they do not, however, prevent the mental fatigue that accompanies repeated experiences of prayer. Even *kavannot* and the best of intentions and preparations are still subject to the powerful grip of boredom. Not only the act but also the preparation for the act can itself become perfunctory. The blessing recited to prepare and inspire us can begin to become just as meaningless as the act that it precedes.

The contemporary Jewish thinker Blu Greenberg offers this perspective for those who find themselves in the stranglehold of religious tedium where even the *kavanna* for a religious act fails to spark the religious imagination:

> But how, the reader might ask, can one perform ritual without perfect and pure intent? Is it not a sham? The answer might be,

"Once more, with feeling." Even so, should ritual or rite happen to be devoid of inner spirit at a given moment, it does not imply that it is devoid of meaning. Sometimes, in ritual, we simply feel part of the community, and that is enough. Sometimes, ritual serves to generate a sense of self, and that is enough. Sometimes, it strengthens the family unit, and that is enough. And sometimes, it connects us to the Divine, and that is enough.[9]

Greenberg reminds us that we do not only perform rituals for a spiritual connection with the Divine. Sometimes we do them to promote cohesion or shared memories within a family. Sometimes we perform rituals to create order and structure in our own lives. Sometimes we do them with the hope that the intention we lack today will surface tomorrow. Thus, our *kavanna* in prayer may fail us in its full theological color but serve in other capacities to strengthen us personally or communally and to keep boredom under control.

Bad Habits

Habituation in prayer or in any ritual behavior is a danger in the realm of the spiritual, and it feeds into boredom powerfully. American psychologist and philosopher William James said of the followers of organized religion that it "has been made for them by others, communicated to them by tradition, determined to fixed forms by imitation, and retained by habit."[10] In this view, "religion consists largely of lifeless dogma maintained through group consensus and social reinforcement."[11] This observation was not James's alone. It was perhaps first made by the ancient Israelite prophets, who railed against the bringing of sacrifices that were empty of true penitence or prayer, a movement of lips without meaning, a habituated behavior that became empty. Isaiah's powerful words rung in the ears of his audience and ours as well:

> *This people draw near with their mouth*
> *And honor Me with their lips,*
> *While their hearts are far from Me,*
> *And their fear of Me is like a command*
> *Carried out by rote. (Isaiah 29:13)*

Rashi, the eleventh-century French exegete Rabbi Shlomo Yitzchaki, understands "rote" here as a failure to worship God with a "complete heart." A later medieval interpreter, Gersonides, adds to Rashi's comments that the individuals found blameworthy in these verses are those who do only what they are narrowly commanded to do and add nothing of themselves, of their own desire and will. It is not that they are being hypocritical, necessarily; they are simply not engaged in what they are doing. They go through the actions but are essentially bored with worship. Their bodies act out the parts, but their hearts "are far" from God. The act of prayer described here lulls the one mouthing it into believing that something is being accomplished when in reality nothing at all is achieved.

The spiritual lethargy described by Isaiah takes a turn for the worse in the last book of Prophets, Malachi. After the prophet Hagai challenges the Israelites to build the Second Temple, even if it cannot match the majesty of the first, the prophet Malachi wonders what went wrong. Echoing God's bald condemnation, Malachi says:

> You ask, "How have we scorned Your name?"
> You offer defiled food on My altar.
> But you ask, "How have we defiled You?"
> By saying, "The table of the Lord can be treated with
>   scorn."
> When you present a blind animal for sacrifice—it
>   doesn't matter.
> When you present a lame or sick one—it doesn't matter.
>   (Malachi 1:6–8)

In this passage, God complains that sacrifices, which are supposed to be offered from the most perfect animals you possess as a sign of gratitude, are replaced by gifts of the lame and the sick. But mediocrity is not the only point of the prophet's outrage. The greater problem is the failure of the Israelites to *recognize* their own spiritual mediocrity. When God says God's altars have been defiled, they retort, "In what way?" They have strayed so much from the path of religious zeal and honor that they can no longer confess a problem because they don't think that it *is* a problem. This is hard-core acedia at its most stubborn, like a stain that several washings cannot remove.

The degree of spiritual lethargy that arises from habituation is one of the most pernicious symptoms of religious boredom precisely because we are so slow to recognize the error of our ways. We think we are doing okay, obeying commandments, acting in community, giving charity, doing what we are told, saying the words, and acting out the motions. It is then that the prophet, in all his tremulousness, cries out:

> *You say, "Oh, what a bother!"*
> *And so you degrade it—said the Lord of Hosts—*
> *and you bring the stolen, the lame, and the sick*
> *and you offer this as a gift.*
> *Will I accept it from you?... (Malachi 1:13)*

The prophet describes the exchange in very human terms that we can understand. At the Temple, the Israelites were obligated to offer something to God, but it felt tiresome, a bother really. The subjects of God's ire feel that they had better things to do but underwent the formulaic steps to perform what was expected or to gain expiation, without feeling or imagination.

Familiarity Breeds Contempt

There is an expression that sums up the prophets' wrath. Psychologists call habituation "declining marginal utility;" in other words, the more we do something, the less appealing it is. There is a remedy, states Harvard psychologist Daniel Gilbert: "Human beings have discovered two devices that allow them to combat this tendency: variety and time. One way to beat habituation is to increase the variety of one's experiences.... Another way to beat habituation is to increase the amount of time that separates repetitions of experience."[12] Gilbert argues that you do not need both variety and time together as factors to minimize habituation. One is sufficient. He even claims that "when episodes are sufficiently separated in time, variety is not only necessary—it can actually be costly."[13]

Within a religious context, rituals frame experience positively when not repeated too frequently and when they offer us a sense of tradition in the repetition. We want to have the same matzah ball soup at every Passover Seder. Passover will not be the same if Aunt Sadie does not make her amazing soup. We will be upset without it. It is both a maker and a marker of tradition. And we need it to help us appreciate the cyclical nature of time and space and reunite us with feelings we once had that were favorable and pleasurable.

Tradition is one positive way to refer to habituation; it is when we do the same thing again and again and are delighted to do so. In a world as fast paced as ours, habituation need not make us nervous. It can actually make us feel highly situated so that we brace the change around us with a core commitment to what securely lies within us.

Holy Insecurity

The search for holiness within Judaism arguably lies in embracing simple, repeated acts and imbuing them with meaning. Habituation is not the problem in this formula; it is the map. Do acts of charity daily, and you will become a charitable person. Withhold your harsh tongue from speaking badly of others every day, and you may find that with the discipline, a nicer, more compassionate self emerges. Pray regularly, and you may have the emotional language to manage pain and express joy, individually and collectively, when it arises.

In a reflective essay on whether Judaism is an optimistic religion, professor and author Shubert Spero writes that Judaism promises what he terms "the joy of trembling" (borrowing Kierkegaard's language):

> This Jewish joy is ... a tempered optimism, a "holy insecurity" which recognizes that existence has meaning under God not *in spite* of its tragedies and sufferings but perhaps *through* its tragedies and sufferings, *by means of* the trivial and the prosaic.... The believing Jew has looked sadness in the face. He knows that

wife, the family, career, the daily tasks are not the ultimate "answer." But precisely because he has accepted their contingency can they have for him freshness and be a source of tempered joy. We can indeed experience the simple joys of life if we know their limitations beforehand. The cry of "vanity of vanities, all is vanity" comes as no surprise because we did not strain the simple joys with a burden they are not equipped to bear.[14]

When we want to achieve something of importance, we are prepared to discipline ourselves; we withstand difficult hours of tedium so that we can complete graduate courses to gain a law degree so that we can practice a profession, earn a living, and support our families. We pound on exercise equipment and perspire because we want to lose a certain amount of weight so that we can fit into our clothes or achieve optimum health. We watch what we eat so that we can nourish our bodies appropriately and maybe live longer and better lives. We learn early on that by restraining our desires, we can achieve certain objectives. The formula is relatively easy; the practice is not.

And yet, in the arena of spiritual growth we often forget this simple formula. Restraint, training, and self-control will yield certain religious benefits that cannot be achieved without discipline. Too often today, we turn to religion to provide a sappy, sweet sentiment to frame a moment in time, like the birth of a child or the last moments of a grandfather's time on this earth. We have let go of Jewish law that seems restrictive and authoritative for something more personally chosen and serendipitously achieved. Judaism begins to look like a bauble, a holiday ornament that is taken off the shelf at certain seasons, dusted, and used when needed—a source of limited joy or familiarity, a comfort that makes no more demands than the back of a shampoo bottle: lather, rinse, repeat. Take out religion from the china cabinet too often and then the problem of habit returns, bringing boredom along with it.

It is not the discipline of Jewish life that makes it boring; sometimes it is the lack of discipline in religious life, the failure to exhibit self-control or filter what we are saying or doing, that creates a Judaism that is devoid of substance.

From Habituation to Discipline

Pirkei Avot (Ethics of the Fathers) 4:1 promotes discipline as a way to achieve true strength: "Who is strong?: One who subdues his passions. As it says: 'One who is slow to anger is better than a hero and one who has control over his will is better than one who conquers a city.'" The Talmud scholar Ben Zoma issued a number of rhetorical questions to surface what human nature is at its best. One of them was redefining strength. Being strong is not a condition of physical might and superiority; strength lies in the ability to conquer passion and resist temptation because even very physically strong individuals fall prey to petty desires.[15]

Rabbi Samson Raphael Hirsch (1808–88), the father of modern German Orthodoxy, comments on the Mishnah (fragment or passage of oral law) that, "The greed for physical pleasure is circumscribed by gratification and satiation." He uses money as an example of the force of temptation. "The striving for money, the *means* for pleasure, has no limit for though money in itself does not give pleasure, it makes possible all future enjoyment. Therefore the lust for money can never be satisfied." At some point, when this seduction reaches excessive levels, people begin to lose the joy in what they have and the pleasure lies only in the pursuit of what is out of reach. In Rabbi Hirsch's words: "Desire no more than you have—and you are indeed rich."

There is nothing original in this thought, or is there? Recent research challenges long-held notions of what develops success in adulthood. Contributing editor at *Wired* and author Jonah Lehrer, in his article "Don't," interviewed Walter Mischel, a Stanford University professor of psychology, on his fascinating experiments with marshmallows.[16]

In the 1960s, in a nursery school/laboratory, Mischel did a series of experiments with young children to see who would be able to resist eating a marshmallow immediately for the gift of two marshmallows a few minutes later. The researcher would leave the room to allow the child more freedom in acting on impulse or waiting. Most children, not surprisingly, consumed marshmallow after marshmallow without stop. The children who waited engaged in many tactics to resist the temptation. Some covered their eyes or turned around so that they wouldn't have to see this fluffy white mound of sugary seduction.

And it worked. Their patience was rewarded. Mischel went back to the students he researched decades later to see how they were doing in life and arrived at some startling conclusions. In the words of Jonah Lehrer:

> For decades, psychologists have focused on raw intelligence as the most important variable when it comes to predicting success in life. Mischel argues that intelligence is largely at the mercy of self-control; even the smartest kids still need to do their homework. "What we're really measuring with the marshmallows isn't willpower or self-control.... It's much more important than that. This task forces kids to find a way to make the situation work for them."

The waiting is not as important as the strategy that the child employs to delay immediate gratification for larger and ultimately more gratifying benefits. That shows intelligence. In fact, one experimental school in Philadelphia that has taken advantage of this research in helping children create strategies to avoid temptation gives students T-shirts that say: "Don't Eat the Marshmallow."

My T-shirt would say: "Don't Eat the Chocolate." I invite you to come up with your own T-shirt wisdom. The point is that Mischel really believes that children can be taught to resist temptation by engaging in certain pre-taught techniques to delay gratification. The point of the exercise is not merely to avoid the dentist, it's to help children learn early that good things really do come to those who wait.

And it's not only children who benefit from this research. True strength lies in discipline, just as Ben Zoma taught two thousand years ago. Is *habituation* just a word that we throw out when we are tired of disciplining ourselves? Do we have the patience and vision to achieve what we really want as our end goals or do we lose sight of the prize because of the big, white marshmallow in front of us?

7 Burnt Out in the Jewish Classroom

Teach us to care and not to care.
Teach us to sit still.

T. S. Eliot

That boredom is primarily seen as a children's "disease" is not hard to understand. We hear our own children or perhaps ourselves as children complaining incessantly of boredom. Long winter school days, interminably extended summer vacations, and rain outside all point the way to hours with nothing to do. And when we, as children, complained, we were often told to rely upon our "inner resources," as I hear myself telling my children now.

Thinking of how ineffective this advice was, I smile. If we were all using our inner resources or had a clue what inner resources meant at ages nine and ten, we might have stimulated them. But we had no idea. We believed that our boredom was someone else's problem, as many adults still feel today. Inner resources? Why should I call upon inner resources if I can relieve boredom by calling upon external stimuli? If someone would just provide a little entertainment, the whole problem would just go away.

The American poet John Berryman (1914–72) captures his boredom with the argument of inner resources in a few sweeping lines:

> And moreover my mother told me as a boy
> (repeatedly) "ever to confess you're bored means you
>   have no
> Inner Resources." I conclude now I have no
> inner resources, because I am heavy bored.[1]

The central figure of our poem makes a confession that no parent can ignore: he has no inner resources with a capital *I* and a capital *R*. In the end, our bored young man agrees with his mother, but what difference does it make? He still has nothing to do. Berryman the poet, it appears, never found real relief for his inner resources, despite winning a Pulitzer Prize for his poetry. Haunted from his childhood by his father's suicide, Berryman took his own life by jumping off the Washington Avenue Bridge in Minneapolis. He missed the water but died anyway. His was one solution to boredom, but not an advisable one.

Not every parent relies on the clarion call of "inner resources" for the occupation of children. Some feel themselves personally responsible for the lack of stimulation their children receive and compensate by overprogramming them, never exposing the children to the fact that boredom can and will exist and that each person must develop some armor or method to manage it. Other parents are not quite as self-sacrificing. A successful Jewish academic reported to me that she can still hear her mother's voice responding to her complaints as a child, "But I have nothing to do," with the formula *"Gey shlog zikh kop in vant"* (Go knock your head against the wall). Hearing this enough times, she came to believe that this was obviously inherited and unoriginal advice.

In the domain of childhood boredom, there is no greater offender than school. "School is boring" is practically a mantra of sacred repetition. You can tell your children to use their inner resources or bang their heads against a wall from today until the cows come home, and it will not change this universal expression of educational tedium. The assumption that school is boring is such a well-accepted norm in the life of children that it need not be articulated; it simply is a fact of childhood to be endured.

This statement is so disturbing that it begs the question of why we have not done more about educational boredom unless we do not take our children seriously when they complain. And yet, we know secretly that they are mostly correct in their assessment, since we may have suffered similarly. I heard a parent once plainly remark that boredom is an important part of education because it prepares students for life. That sets the expectations awfully low. Should we regard school as an institution that educates us for a lifetime of nonactivity, lack of interest, mental fatigue, and intellectual listlessness? School becomes, in this equation, a curiosity killer.

This reality is nowhere better played out than in afternoon Hebrew schools across the United States and beyond. Beyond a doubt, Hebrew school is much worse on the boredom scale than regular school because it happens after an already long day of tiring classes, is often forced upon students, and usually involves less-creative techniques taught by less-experienced teachers. Most children fail to find it relevant to their lives, and it will make no difference to their grade point averages for college acceptance or be measured with any outside metrics. Thus, in addition to seeming irrelevant, it has the added "bonus" of not being necessary in terms of later school success, and so there really is no incentive to combat boredom. Having suffered myself, I took great amusement in a short story where the young protagonist tells his father that he hates Hebrew school, to which his father congratulates him and tells him that he is following a fine family tradition, since he hated Hebrew school himself, as did his father. *Mazel tov.* We have successfully produced generations of bored Hebrew schoolers. If that's not tradition, then what is?

The fact that we have tolerated this poor state of educational affairs for so long is simply remarkable. In the time that generations of students have been hating Hebrew school, we have survived the Holocaust, drained swamps to build the State of Israel, and become one of the most affluent and influential minorities in virtually every host country in the Diaspora. As a people, we are highly overrepresented as Nobel Prize winners. As revolutionaries we can claim the biblical Abraham, Moses, Rabbi Yochanan Ben Zakai, Albert Einstein, Niles Bohr, Sigmund Freud, and Karl Marx, to list only a few, but we have yet to apply Jewish genius to revolutionize Jewish education. For some reason, we have not made Jewish boredom in the classroom important enough to do something about it.

Jewish Success

As a Jewish community, this accepted norm is not tenable. Jews have enjoyed high rates of literacy for centuries. School was seen and continues to be regarded as a critical building block for later success. A Jewish mother I met recently shared with me that she let her children do almost anything they wanted growing up; they consumed sugar-filled cereals, came home late, had all kinds of friends. "The only rule in my house was: do your homework. It's the only thing I ever cared about." And because tuition for Jewish day schools, Hebrew schools, and university education requires so many parental sacrifices, parents are wise to convince their children that homework is important. But if boredom is so pervasive in our classrooms, we are not getting a good return on our investment. We may not be giving children an opportunity to see the riches of our tradition or are educating them just badly enough to help them walk away from thousands of years of Jewish history.

The Boredom Muscle

We are not culturally isolated in this issue. Today, boredom in the classroom is treated the way many other child-related issues are treated, as an external problem implicating school administrators, teachers, and textbooks. It is symptomatic of a popular way of parenting, rather than educating, today, which has been called hover parenting, helicopter parenting, overparenting, or monster parenting. I tend to think of it as parenting as a sport, usually an extreme sport.

Wendy Mogul, a well-known clinical psychologist and author, helps us understand what we've done wrong in *The Blessing of a Skinned Knee*:

> Parents have a paradoxical mission. We have to work hard not to provide our children with interesting things to do. Children need a chance to build up their boredom tolerance muscle. If you adopt an "I know you'll find something to do soon" attitude and think of boredom as a positive opportunity instead of something to be gotten rid of, children have a better chance of learning how to entertain themselves. Treat daydreaming and fooling around as valuable activities. Being messy, noisy, silly, goofy and vegging-out are as essential to the development of your child's mind and spirit as anything else he does.[2]

Overprogramming our children, both in school and out, and pressuring them to use every moment toward the accomplishment of some futuristic goal generates boredom because children begin to detach from the learning process and only care about the outcomes that we put forward, rather than self-determined educational goals that arise from natural curiosity.

As parents, we also live in a self-esteem culture where we may tell our children that they are perfect or at least very, very exceptional and hover over them; bad grades are sometimes met with a reprimand to the teacher or at least a question of his or her competency. We can stand over our children so that they do not fall, do not get bruised, do not feel obligated to others who do not affirm their own sense of self. And we wonder about a growing sense of entitlement in our emerging generation of young people. Children need to learn to manage bad teachers and subjects that are not interesting; it is a life skill.

The "boredom tolerance muscle" indeed needs to be built up but built up through children themselves so that they begin to think creatively about their time, rather than refuse parental suggestions or tire parents out who are trying too hard to come up with suggestions to counter their children's boredom.

A Video Game Warning

A word here about technology: beware the TV or video game as a "solution" to boredom. These tools are often used as babysitters and boredom fillers because most kids enjoy them and they provide parents with some much needed time to get their own work, errands, or exercising done. Children accept this offer of free screen time with willingness instead of the usual rejection of parental suggestions; it is an easy recommendation when the cries of "I'm bored" become intolerable. Electronic gadgets rarely have to be plied on children; they usually have to be peeled away from their anxious clutches.

This is a problematic way to curb boredom in children, not only because of the content ambivalence that many parents have about video and TV violence, language, or its educational message or lack of one. Screen time is isolating from social play, and it locks the imagination into one form of release, not allowing boredom to generate creative ideas. As with the religious boredom mentioned earlier, child boredom is an important stimulant to play.

Imagine a tech-free day for a moment. Your child complains about this decree ferociously: "I'm bored. I have nothing to do if you don't let me watch TV. Okay, I'll just sit here and do nothing." Do not be taken in by these idle threats. A stubborn child may sit on the couch for a few minutes pouting but will soon begin to seek out options to fill time. Using effortless time fillers like video games prevents children from developing the mental muscle to handle boredom, as Mogul well advises, and may take away from the rich gift that children can give themselves: the knowledge that they have the personal capacity to relieve boredom. Many of the most rewarding games we played as children came out of a stretch of boredom that seemed interminable at the time but led to creating magic potions, building secret hideouts, playing house, making up plays, celebrating Barbie weddings, wrestling, and challenging each other to Monopoly marathons.

Preparation for Life

The assumption that school will be boring goes unchallenged perhaps because there are no easy solutions and because it may reflect a much larger cultural assumption about life generally and about Jewish life specifically. Do we educate in a boring manner because life is ultimately a reflection of our education? Sean Desmond Healy, the thinker we encountered earlier, comments on this very problem:

> Considering how pervasive anyone familiar with schools must know it to be, it is quite remarkable how little attention is given to boredom of any sort in the vast literature, and subliterature, of education. It is perhaps just taken for granted that it will be prevalent and does not matter or, by the more optimistic, that it is part of the school's business to get their clients used to what is so much a part of the outside world, training in reality or, by the more ignorant, that it does not exist there in any significant measure.[3]

In other words, school *does* indeed prepare us for life, a life of boredom and limited expectations by manufacturing an environment that produces prolonged tolerance for a lack of stimulation.

What is learned so often in school corridors and libraries is a dulling of the senses. At its worst, school teaches us through all of its implicit messaging that curiosity, self-satisfaction, meaning, amusement, and self-knowledge are to be found elsewhere, somewhere outside the classroom, if they are to be found at all. Healy, again, stimulates our conversation further:

> Boredom in school, as elsewhere, is of course nothing new in itself, but its growth and its intensification derive from the sense that students—and increasingly teachers, too—have that, to some extent inevitable, tedium and grind of study and learning, and the prolonged subordination to authority, are no longer really worth it; or that, while they may be unavoidable en route to the desired goals, they are little more than hurdles that have to be jumped in order to satisfy the bureaucratic and largely meaningless requirements of absurd institutions. Earlier ... students in school had a firm sense that whatever they had to go through was somehow *intrinsically* worthwhile, even if it was dreary and distasteful. It fitted in with what people everywhere and consistently held to be true, right and desirable, and if one found it otherwise, then the fault lay in oneself and not in the system.[4]

When school ceases to feel intrinsically worthwhile but is only a set of obstacles to be overcome, then students do the minimum required to suffer through it because it is only a means to an end.

As educators and parents, we may support this approach and attitude by emphasizing grades rather than learning, standardized testing rather than curiosity, and next steps rather than present engagement. We teach that doing well at any stage of education is important because it will help secure a prized place in the next institution, leading to a successful career and a presumed happy life. Instead, we need to emphasize the value of the moment of learning and teach toward it.

Think of Jewish education specifically. Much of Hebrew school is geared toward basic bar and bat mitzvah competency. For too many parents, as long as their young teens can competently get through a weekend of standard ritual and an elaborate party, they have ostensibly completed what they came to school for in the first place. This naturally contributes to the sense that at thirteen it is time to say goodbye. While Jewish day school content assumes and expects more, the endgame is different in nature but not different in its futuristic outlook. Laws not always relevant to a child's particular stage in life are taught because there may not be a future opportunity, like detailed laws of Jewish family purity, *kashrut* (keeping kosher), and Shabbat. Ironically, because we are overly concerned with future observance, we minimize current relevancy, and then students often do not ever get to future observance because they find the material they studied in high school irrelevant.

I have spoken to numerous students who took a gap year or several months between high school and college to pursue higher Judaic knowledge in academies in Israel or an Israel experience, what is colloquially referred to as "a year off." If anything, it was the first year many of them had "on"; they traveled, picked carrots on a kibbutz, or sat in study halls of their own choice and studied without grades or external measures and goals. The objective was simply personal spiritual and intellectual growth and understanding. And because those factors mattered more than any others, they did what we are not doing enough of in Jewish schools. They learned something. They found esoteric subjects interesting, when the same subject taught in high school did nothing to whet an intellectual appetite. Many such graduates report that as a result of a year off studying Talmud, the Hebrew Bible, and Jewish law, they became better college students, lawyers, doctors, and parents. Why? Because they cared about the educational present and were not always looking beyond the classroom to somewhere else.

Looking Beyond the Problem

Within Jewish education, boredom, when it exists, is often attributable to three factors: (1) unexceptional, uninspiring, or inexperienced teachers; (2) little interactivity or a non-child-centered approach; and (3) a lack of concern for subject relevance.

We have all had boring teachers. Some of us specialized in them. Even as I write this, the face of a science teacher and an English professor comes to mind. The boredom may have to do with the monotone of a teacher's voice, his or her inability to make the subject interesting, or a slow pace of learning that involves constant repetition on the teacher's part. Often teachers who bore are themselves bored, with the subject or their job or their students. Just like the students who feel they are forced to attend class, bored teachers may feel that they have little choice but to get through the end of the day and bring home a paycheck. As the old adage goes, "The notes of the teachers become the notes of the students without passing through the heads of either."

Often what stays with a student long after the facts, figures, and blackboard notations have been erased is the passion or lack of it that a teacher has for a subject or the sense of curiosity and wonder that the teacher communicates about learning in general. At a teacher's best, the love of subject, love of teaching, and love of people work with a wonderful confluence to create mastery in the classroom, but this synergy cannot always be expected. A teacher who does not have a passion for his or her subject will always bore students, since no amount of love for people alone can sustain a forty-five-minute discussion on a particular topic. And a love of subject without care for the students' interest will never an interesting teacher make.

The problem of teachers who are not passionate about their subject or students, are inexperienced, or are themselves bored flows into the second problem afflicting students in Jewish classrooms: a lack of interactivity or a non-child-centered approach. This is a difficult problem to tackle in traditional Jewish education, where respect and admiration for rabbis and teachers are very high; indeed, one who teaches a child is considered in the abstract philosophical sense to be a parent to that very child, augmenting respect for the teacher as a primal authority figure in a child's life. We do not put the child first as much as we do the intellectual capabilities of the teacher. In Jewish law, students are supposed to rise for teachers, confess their disrespect for teachers on Yom Kippur, our holiest of days, and not recite Jewish law in front of a teacher, even if at some future time the knowledge of the student surpasses that of the teacher.

Letting Go in the Classroom

Our third issue with boredom in the classroom is that of relevance, making students feel that their learning has something to do with their lives. This can only happen when learning is more child-centered. We cannot be the sole determinants of what someone else feels is relevant, even and especially children.

The transition to child-centered study in an ancient and revered tradition of education does not come easy, but we should take comfort in the fact that it has not come easy to anyone in the field. Observe the following recollections of a veteran teacher who readjusted her teaching style and describes the difficulty of doing so:

> I think most people who go into teaching are not risk-takers. We had positive experiences with school. We are pleasers; we play the game. We like controlled situations and are not comfortable making mistakes. We do the right thing so that we have stellar evaluations from administrators.
>
> To be part of the revolution, I must be in control of my classes without it being a controlled situation.... I must trust my students enough to let them out of their seats and to make mistakes of their own, a scary thought in some of my classes.... We have done a great disservice to these students by making them more concerned with their grades than their education. I'm not sure how to turn these students around.... The transition from teacher-centered to student-centered learning is tough. My students, not I, must become the masters of my kingdom/ classroom. Neither I, my students, my administrators nor my lessons are accustomed to this shift of control.[5]

Students are not bored when they are given greater ownership of their learning. This is not suggesting that they teach themselves or that the classroom is a place of unstructured chaos. But when their curiosity is not central to the learning process, then teachers become like the parents mentioned earlier, solely responsible for the "edutainment" of children and solely responsible for their boredom.

Mari Clayton Glamser, the teacher who authored the article from which the quote is excerpted, singles out honor roll students as particularly inflexible and unwilling to take control of their learning. This may come as a surprise to some readers, but it should not. Strong students in the classroom are often those who follow rules, do as the teacher says, and do not stray far from the intellectual path set by others. Literary essayist Nassim Nicholas Taleb, author of *The Black Swan: The Impact of the Highly Improbable*, confirms this in an unlikely diatribe on intelligence:

> A nerd is simply someone who thinks exceedingly inside the box. Have you ever wondered why so many of these straight-A students end up going nowhere in life while someone who lagged behind is now getting the shekels, buying the diamond and getting his phone calls returned? Or even getting the Nobel Prize...? Some of this may have something to do with luck in outcomes, but there is the sterile and obscurantist quality that is often associated with classroom knowledge that may get in the way of understanding what's going on in real life.[6]

Taleb creates two different student personalities and demonstrates why the one who was outdone in an IQ test might outperform the "good" student in life because, despite gaps in his learning and acquisition of culture, he has "an enormous curiosity about the texture of reality, and his own erudition [is] ... more scientific in the literal, though not in the social sense."[7]

The learning that takes place outside of school that gives this type of real-world advantage, need not take place outside the walls of the classroom. It just requires a different kind of classroom. I found this out myself only in the last stages of my own graduate education. For my entire school career, I carefully followed instructions, sought the approval of my teachers, and tried to please them by doing what they demanded. As I spent more time in graduate school, I began to see that the very tools that brought me success on report cards through adolescence and college got in the way of academic achievement in the upper echelons. I was not creative and feisty enough. I was too afraid to challenge authority, take control of my learning, and defend my ideas stridently. Many tenured professors I observed had a certain aggressive hunger that fed their careers and made their research startlingly original. I realized that school had precisely not prepared me for the highest levels of my education.

Higher Learning

Glamser discusses the difficulties of finding the right balance between basic teaching and lecturing skills and student autonomy. She talks about the importance of support in this method and all about learning its boundaries. Teachers in this model are expert facilitators and knowledge experts who can help guide, shape, and mold discussion without ruling the class. They understand that by letting go of control, they ultimately and actively hand it over to others without absolving all in the room of control and creating anarchy.

This is a challenge in the Jewish classroom, as it is in every classroom. It may be a greater challenge in the Hebrew school classroom, where teachers struggle with time constraints and many are not teachers by vocation; classroom management seems burdensome and difficult. But if you only have an hour a week, why not make it one where the students take charge of their learning in the present rather than teachers pushing information for the future that has little relevance for the present? It is this initial negative exposure to learning about Judaism that often creates profound alienation from Judaism. Healy observes:

> It is all too obvious, looking at what is usually called the traditional school ... that education, far from assisting in the essential task of discovering and working with reality, one's own and that of the world, is all too often one of the major culprits in the process of alienating man from being.[8]

No knowledge of Judaism may be infinitely preferable to alienation; at least ignorance usually produces neutrality and sometimes receptivity to learning. Alienation brings about neither outcome.

Boredom in Adult Education

Although this is a chapter on children and boredom, let us digress for a moment, while we are on the subject of education, to talk about the adult classroom. The conundrum of learning just discussed, inverting the roles of teachers and students to achieve learning and engagement, is necessary not only in the child's classroom. Its absence is legion in the adult educational setting as well. Many adults who come back to study Judaism as Hebrew school dropouts find themselves insecure and untried in the field of Jewish studies. They may be attending a synagogue class or one of the excellent two-year programs of Jewish studies available nationally and internationally based on Jewish text study in biblical exegesis, history, Talmud, and philosophy. If they enter the room at all, they do so with baby steps.

I often have a class full of well-accomplished adult students who balk the first day at their own ignorance. What is exegesis? Will we have homework? Will I understand the readings? I don't know anything. They raise their hands tentatively and confess that they are going to ask a stupid question. When I say that there is no such thing as a stupid question, they do not believe me; they are definitely the exception to the rule. Jewish adult learners need to be given enormous encouragement and support when they jump start their studies after a long hiatus and a rusty first class. They need to be commended for taking chances and coming back to "school" after having an initially bad experience as kids, as so many of my students share with their new friends.

Adults do not need to be lectured to as if they were in a graduate school class of hundreds with minimal participation; it is tempting to take total control because so often adult students offer it willingly to the teacher. "You're the expert. You talk. No one needs to hear me. I don't know anything." Resist this temptation as a teacher or as a student because it can easily become an invitation to passive learning and distraction. Adult students are generally more polite and are there of their own accord, anxious to learn. But that zeal must be appropriately nurtured so that they feel in charge of their learning, just as they control so many areas and decisions in other aspects of their lives. Adults value autonomy in their learning.

We mentioned subject relevance and return to it as a problem in the adult classroom. As mentioned earlier, a Judaic curriculum often focuses on areas of Jewish law or history that feel either too ancient or outdated for many students. The questions and issues that students wrestle with at their specific stage of development are the ones that interest them most, that make Judaism seem real, alive, and a source of wisdom for areas that engage their uppermost thoughts. Teachers can only discover what students care about by allowing them a voice in determining the course of their learning, to some degree.

This can be achieved in any number of ways; the specifics or the "what" of the matter concerns us less than the "why" and the "how," which should preoccupy every educator.[9] The "why" must ultimately be about wisdom and not information; today, with the power of the Internet, most questions about Judaism can be answered with the click of a computer button. To make studying Judaism in a classroom worthwhile, there must be something magical about the student-teacher relationship and something dynamic about the learning process that helps students see Judaism as a source and reservoir of positive associations.

Many of my adult students come to class after limited forays into Buddhism or other Far Eastern traditions of faith and wisdom. They moved in that direction before examining the spiritual traditions of their own birth faith because these other traditions seemed to hold more promise of personal spiritual growth. Their associations with Judaism and Jewish people were largely about food, material wealth, and overachievement.

The Soul of Education

What concerns us here is the residual impact of early Jewish study that is irrelevant to future choices about Jewish education and Jewish living.

How can we ensure that Jewish learning is sufficiently compelling that the material and methods are relevant and the residual impact is positive? We have to believe, against the tide of skepticism, that this can indeed be achieved. According to educator John Holt:

> Almost all children are bored in school. Why shouldn't they be? We would be.... Very little in school is exciting and meaningful.... We [must] begin where schools hardly ever do begin, by recognizing that the daily lives of these children are the most real and meaningful things they know. Why not begin their education there? It can be done.[10]

When what is learned becomes "exciting and meaningful," the residual impact of Jewish education is powerful and compels children and adults to learn and explore further. What makes the study of Judaism relevant is the way it shapes personal identity, a tall order for any kind of learning, but what also colors our associations with a subject as a source of wisdom. As writer and philosopher Michel de Montaigne puts it elegantly:

> I gladly come back to the theme of the absurdity of our education: its end has not been to make us good and wise, but learned. And it has succeeded. It has not taught us to seek virtue and to embrace wisdom: it has impressed upon us their derivation and their etymology.... We readily inquire, "Does she know Greek or Latin? Can he write poetry or prose?" But what matters most is what we put last: "Has he become better or wiser?" We ought to find out not who understands most but who understands best. We work merely to fill the memory, leaving the understanding and the sense of right and wrong empty.[11]

School is, as an institution, the great transmitter of social values and one of the most powerful shapers of personal identity, either as a tool of obedience to cultural expectations or in reaction to those expectations. Sometimes the great transmitter of values becomes merely a game of failed or ascertained expectations, not turning out a student who is "better or wiser," or to use a term from Yiddish, not producing a *mensch*.

Great Expectations

Bored students sit in anticipated detachment, or worse, withdrawal from learning and even from the social construction that is the classroom. Healy believes that school environments should present opportunities for self-knowledge:

> If the self *is* to be grasped in its irreality, education must be one long campaign against the forces of illusions and reality, forces that seek, especially in our society for one reason or another, to overwhelm or to subvert it and suborn it. And the prospects of success do not look encouraging, not least because of the ubiquity and subtlety of the influences dedicated to diverting man from his true central concerns, and the fact that they operate on the individual from his earliest days. Against these forces the schools might act—but by and large do not—as some sort of counterpoise.[12]

American philosopher, psychologist, and educational reformer John Dewey, in his classic *Education and Experience*, reveals the chasm that separates children from authentic learning by showing the distance between traditional schooling and actual learning:

> The traditional scheme is, in essence, one of imposition from above and from outside. It imposes adult standards, subject-matter, and methods upon those who are only growing slowly toward maturity. The gap is so great that the required subject-matter, the methods of learning and of behaving are foreign to the existing capacities of the young ... the gulf between the mature or adult products and the experience and abilities of the young is so wide that the very situation forbids much active participation by pupils in the development of what is taught.[13]

The gap is where real learning takes place. The top-down method of traditional education leads to boredom precisely because the child does not have the tools or resources to respond to adult standards. When Jewish teaching works its magic, it is getting at the root of human existence and forcing us to examine ourselves and the world through a different prism.

A Sacred Prism

Professor of Jewish education Michael Rosenak understands that for boredom to leave the Jewish classroom, it is critical to probe the issue of relevance: "What is essential to any sacred book and actually defines it as sacred is that, in one way or another, it raises ultimate questions and makes its readers view these questions as "deep."[14] Rosenak then offers us a template of questions that sacred texts should stimulate us to ask when Jewish education is working at its best:

1. Who am I, really?
2. What is and what should be most important to me?
3. How should I live my life, with myself and with others?
4. What can I know?
5. And what is most important to know?
6. Where did it all start?
7. Where is it all going?
8. ... *Where am I in my life?*[15]

Not all educational experiences can or should stimulate these questions or the classroom might look like a cross between a synagogue and a psychologist's office, but religious education is not only or exclusively for the purpose of information. This is often a stumbling block for teachers within Jewish institutions. They impart information about religious traditions, Hebrew language, or Jewish history without engaging in questions of personal meaning. If I do not know why I need to know this, perhaps I will not bother knowing it, thinks that disengaged mind of the student. If we can provide students with a why that is a meaningful why for them, then the how will follow. Without the why, the how will never be of interest.

Education and Originality

The tradition of asking good questions is as old as the Passover Seder. Out of the four sons of the Seder, the wise child is the one who asks a very specific question about Jewish law. The fourth child is the one who does not even know how to ask a question so that we must ask him one to stimulate some thought, any thought, about the Exodus story. Jewish accomplishment is regarded in the way that we ask questions, not deliver answers. The most pitied student is the one who cannot even ask a question. Nevertheless, everyone still has a place at the table.

Within traditional Jewish educational settings like yeshivot and study halls, there is a high value placed on *hiddush*, an original thought, literally translated as something new or revelatory. No better technique attacks boredom in the classroom than asking and prompting good questions. Precocious children in yeshiva settings were often told to ask good questions and were praised or criticized on the merit of their questions. Did they ask a question that would reveal deep or detailed knowledge of a subject that would surface some kind of genius to be detected by the teacher, the *melamed*?

It is the stimulation of the question itself that tells us a great deal about a child's intellectual maturity or potential. What is a question other than an act of involvement? You can give an answer and be bored and disengaged, but to ask a really good question, you must be involved and even enthralled by what you are learning. Professor of philosophy Noam Zohar, in the marginalia of his Haggadah *A Different Night*, tells of a Jewish Nobel laureate in science who, upon leaving for school every morning as a child, was told by his parent to ask good questions. Quite a different approach than "Have fun" or "Have a nice day." The idea of asking a good question, a powerful question, is the key to intellectual development and may one day land you with a Nobel Prize.

Boredom and Good Questions

The novelist and literary critic Cynthia Ozick cites the philosopher Suzanne K. Langer, who observed that "every answer is concealed in the question that elicits it, and that what we must strive to do, then, is not look for the right answer, but attempt rather to discover the right question."[16] The right question creates an intellectual moment of revelation that may lead to an original answer, a *hiddush*. A *hiddush*, an intellectual novelty, was and still is the prize of Talmudic study. It is the jackpot of Jewish intellectual accomplishments. It tells others in a classroom that they are sitting in the presence of greatness. After all, to come up with a new thought on a document that is close to two thousand years old and has been commented on for nearly as long is a mighty accomplishment indeed.

At a certain stage in Jewish history, intellectual boredom was fought through *pilpul*, Talmudic casuistry. These are intricate connections made by a student who is able to merge together different commentaries and the original text and perhaps multiple passages of Talmud into a seamless intellectual unit, stringing and weaving together concepts on different subjects into an intellectually integrated whole. Hermeneutically, the student who flexes his intellectual muscle in *pilpul* often steers far away from the literal meaning of verses and laws to achieve this unified whole, but no matter, it relieved the boredom that can creep up on even the most passionate Talmud student and can help raise the esteem in which the student is held by others, as well as generate pride in himself.

Pilpul, however, has a checkered history in Jewish educational thought. Not everyone was enamored of it because the word games and wordplays took students away from literal meanings or so engaged them in their own quest for *hiddush* that they failed in the bread-and-butter understanding of texts. Great Rabbis of the sixteenth century warned teachers of the dangers of *hiddush*, almost assuring them that students needed the rote and regular study of Talmud to keep them on the straight and narrow. In other words, there is a hidden danger in making education interesting and clever all of the time. On the one hand, we risk boredom when we do not stress novelty. On the other hand, when we stress educational novelty, we run the danger of not managing expectations properly and not teaching anyone the fundamentals of a subject.

Boredom occurs when we run out of questions because it demonstrates that we have run out of interest. Combating boredom in the Jewish classroom, or any classroom for that matter, is ultimately about the stimulation of questions. Returning to the Seder table, that ancient classroom of Jewish history, we find that Maimonides encouraged us to place objects, educational props, on the table and to use the complexity of the Haggadah "to make the children ask." The purpose of Passover is not to tell our children the story of Jewish peoplehood; it is to make the evening interesting enough for them to ask questions. Telling, especially repeated telling, leads to a flat story with a dull landscape. Asking leads to exploration, further questioning, engagement, creativity. Boredom will only leave the classroom when we have done a good enough job of making "the children ask."

8

Boredom and Wonder

Those who wonder discover that
this in itself is wonder.

M. C. Escher

English politician Sir Winston Churchill did not begin painting until the age of forty, and his late-life discovery of talent was clearly a source of inspiration and wonder for him. In his slim and wonderful little guide to painting, Churchill offers an insight into why hobbies are so important and what art did to stimulate him and take his mind off the stresses of political life. He begins his analysis with observations on the nature of people: "Broadly speaking, human beings may be divided into three classes: those who are toiled to death, those who are worried to death, and those who are bored to death."[1]

To manage these conditions, Churchill recommends that people adopt two to three hobbies to combat the stressful effects of toil, worry, and boredom. For this English statesman, nothing worked its wonders more than a change of attention:

> Change is the master key. A man can wear out a particular part of his mind by continually using it and tiring it, just the same way as he can wear out the elbows of his coat. There is, however, this difference between the living cells of the brain and inanimate articles: one cannot mend the frayed elbows of a coat by rubbing the sleeves and the shoulders; but the tired parts of

the mind can be rested and strengthened, not merely by rest, but by using other parts.[2]

The image of a coat worn thin at the elbows is an apt metaphor for boredom, since boredom wears us down through continual demands made on that which has become overused or overfamiliar. But in looking at a coat, we might discover that although the elbows need patching, the rest of the garment is actually quite passable. Had we taken greater care, we may have more evenly distributed the wear and stretched the use of the coat for longer. Our minds, according to Churchill, can be repaired much easier than the fray of tweed with a little stimulation to parts previously unused.

Unpacking the metaphor, we find Churchill's words reassuring. Boredom happens when we overuse one part of our mental or physical energies and let other parts atrophy, perhaps not even realizing their capacity for use. Churchill almost giggles with giddy enthusiasm as he shares with his readers the revelation of his latent artistic talent:

> To have reached the age of forty without ever handling a brush or fiddling with a pencil, to have regarded with mature eye the painting of pictures of any kind as a mystery, to have stood agape before the chalk of the pavement artist, and then suddenly to find oneself plunged in the middle of a new and intense form of interest and action with paints and palettes and canvases, and not to be discouraged by results, is an astonishing and enriching experience.[3]

Churchill surprised himself. He also shares the moment that he tentatively put his first oils on canvas, gingerly placing a small amount of paint in a limited amount so as not to mar the blank canvas overly much. Not until a gifted friend came by the canvas, asked for a brush, and used large blue brushstrokes to cover her own canvas did Churchill realize that the canvas was grinning at him. "The spell was broken. The sickly inhibitions rolled away. I seized the largest brush and fell upon my victim with berserk fury. I have never felt any awe of a canvas since."[4] Fearing failure, he did not initially want to take a risk, but with the encouragement of a friend, Churchill began to approach the canvas more boldly, discovering something remarkable about himself at the same time.

The Human Condition

Churchill's foray into art stimulated intense feelings of wonder, and the experience gave rise to larger, abstract questions about the human condition. We envy Churchill for his sense of wonder, and if we could bottle it, we might stop boredom in its very tracks. In that bottle of wonder, we would find astonishment, admiration, awe, marvel, curiosity, or surprise at that which is novel.

We have spent a lot of time thinking about boredom but not about wonder, arguably its antonym. Professor and author Robert C. Fuller, in his book *Wonder: From Emotion to Spirituality*, suggests that wonder has an open-ended freshness to it; it is an attitude that amplifies patterns and harmony to create a unifying sense of our connection to others, to nature, and to God:

> Wonder excites our ontological imagination in ways that enhance our capacity to seek deeper patterns in the universe.... It entices us to entertain the possibility that our highest fulfillment might require adapting ourselves to a metaphysical reality. Yet, on the other hand, wonder encourages an open-ended or heuristic approach to life. It thus imbues personal spirituality with a fresh quality.[5]

Fuller asks us to view wonder as a freshness or an openness that expands our capacity to take in the universe, what is both known and unknown.

The Divine Mystery

Traditionally, religion has always dealt with areas of *mysterium tremendum*: the elusive and lofty, the transcendental and incomprehensible. Even Nietzsche had to admit that religion had the capacity to still boredom because it offered a structure of meaning:

> The founders of religion [realized the need] to post a particular
> kind of life and everyday customs that have the effect of a *disci-*
> *plina voluntatis* and at the same time banish boredom—and
> then to bestow on this lifestyle an *interpretation* that makes it
> appear to be illuminated by the highest value.[6]

One explanation for boredom's impressive power is that it saps the mystery out of the universe. Nothing feels new or unique or incomprehensible. Nothing is mysterious anymore. The media, especially reality TV,
gossip magazines, and newspapers, have blown the lid off people and
events. There is less aura around political candidates, government figures, and celebrities because we are seemingly told everything about
them. Even in the realm of geography, television has managed to show
us so many parts of the world, we can't help but wonder whether TV has
minimized the mystique of travel. As Fuller remarks:

> The world becomes boring when everything is transparent.
> That is why people hanker for what is dangerous and shock-
> ing. They have replaced the non-transparent by the
> extreme.... The chaos and violence is what moves one from
> boredom to life, awakening oneself. Providing life with some
> sort of meaning. Wonder prompts us to consider how particu-
> larly vivid displays of vitality, beauty, or power might reveal a
> purpose or intentionality of the universe as a whole. As such,
> wonder stimulates efforts to discern what is of intrinsic value or
> meaning (as opposed to what is of utilitarian value or mean-
> ing). And it consequently elicits efforts to find a harmonious
> relationship with, rather than active mastery of, our wider sur-
> roundings.[7]

When we feel wonder, we engage our sense of curiosity to the fullest.
Fuller counteracts this transparency by making a plea for mystery:

> Wonder is not only an emotion that stimulates us to look at
> something more expansively, it is also the end product of that

examination. I may be at the beach, marveling at the vastness of creation, and suddenly experience a deep attachment to nature's beauty. As I pause to reflect on nature with the sound of the waves in the background, I feel an intense connectivity with the world and wonder at the perfection of the God who created oceans and then experience a need to thank God for this gift.[8]

Wonder is both an emotion in and of itself and a catalyst to other emotions. Wonder is generated not only by the vastness of nature; we may marvel most at some compact treasure that keys us into the complex and intricate workings of God and nature. Astonishment leads to more astonishment. Curiosity begets more curiosity. We begin to understand how wonder is grander than a momentary response to beauty but is itself a spiritual approach to living.

A Jewish Approach to Wonder

Looking at Judaism directly, we find not only compelling examples of the way in which wonder shapes Jewish law and custom, but we also find an experience of wonder that is a primary and fundamental expression of Judaism.

According to Rabbinic tradition, Judaism was founded not through an act of revelation but through an act of wonder. According to Maimonides and earlier Sages, Abraham actually discovered Judaism. Weaving together Talmudic statements and observations with Maimonides' own blend of Aristotelianism, this medieval Jewish philosopher creates a portrait of Abraham as a seeker, a man of unbounded curiosity, who, just as the above paragraph describes, saw vivid displays of power and beauty that brought him to ponder the workings of the universe. All pointed to one Creator and away from Abraham's ancestral beginnings: his father's idol-making profession. In this reading, Abraham looked at the stars and planets, asked how it was that they could be suspended in space without any divine driver, and arrived at a conclusion based on scientific inquiry that God, one God, must exist.[9] According to Maimonides:

When that great one [Abraham] was weaned, he began to ponder and reflect—while he was but a child—and he began to
think day and night, and he was bewildered: How is it possible that this planet spins continuously without one to position and drive it? Who turns it? It cannot be that it would
turn on its own. He had no teacher nor one who advised him
of anything, rather he was immersed in Ur-Casdim amongst
idol-worshippers and fools; his father and mother and the
nation were all idol-worshippers, and he worshipped with
them. But he questioned and began to understand until he
achieved the true path and he contemplated justice from deep
perception and finally concluded that there is one God who
turns the planets and who created everything and that there
is no other God beside Him. And he knew that the whole
world was mistaken and understood what led them to their
error.... And Abraham was forty years old when he came to
know his Maker.[10]

Maimonides' marvelous description depicts a boy struggling against his
social environs with profound intellectual questions about the world
that others simply did not ask. His curiosity did not let him rest. He
wrestled with large, shattering questions and emerged an iconoclast with
the courage of conviction to question his family, his community, and the
religious doctrines of his day.

In the Midrash, Rabbinic homilies on the Bible, Abraham did
more than arrive at the notion of monotheism; he entered his father's
idol shop, smashed the idols, a remarkable and fitting image for an *iconoclast*, and then, in an act of irony, placed the hammer in the hands of
the idol itself. When his father returned to see his wares in pieces,
Abraham blamed the idol who wielded the hammer in his inanimate,
statuesque pose. Abraham's father was outraged at his son and told him
that the act was impossible. Abraham had the perfect conclusion to a
day's spiritual work when he retorted that if an idol is not capable of
destroying other idols, did it have any power at all? The stories and leg-
ends that surround Abraham's early years invest Abraham with the

qualities of wonder: a mix of curiosity, rationality, marvel, tenacity, and finally the courage to spread his views by challenging his detractors on their own terms.

Creating Possibilities

Wonder opens possibilities that, in turn, opens more possibilities, expanding and enhancing experience and thought, as Fuller comments:

> Wonder, like heightened interest, momentarily suspends habitual ways of looking at the world and instead lures people into new and creative engagement with their surroundings. Rather than encouraging behaviors that distance us from our environment, wonder induces receptivity and openness. It prompts us to become more connected with the wider environment.[11]

This passage perfectly explains the trajectory of Abraham's thinking. Wonder took him out of the habitual way that his family and tribe viewed worship; he began a creative engagement with his natural surroundings that led him on a path of discovery that distanced him from his past and made him receptive to an entirely new future. And, most important, it was not the wonder of a moment that made the difference. It was sustained wonder, a wonder that was activated over more than three decades of questioning, that led to his startling conclusion, his "aha" moment.

It is funny how Churchill discovered something about himself at forty, and Abraham discovered something about the world at forty. This happy coincidence illustrates the aphorism in *Pirkei Avot* (Ethics of the Fathers) 5:25, "Forty is for wisdom." Maturity, growth, intellectual development, and curiosity are not elementary school qualities in Judaism; they represent a long-standing commitment to astonishment that begins young yet fully germinates in midlife into remarkable depth perception. Forget midlife crisis. With sufficient curiosity, midlife is the time you really begin to live.

From Reason and Revelation to Momentary Awe

In Rabbinic literature, Abraham's questioning represented a level of sustained astonishment until he found theosophic treasure. But Jewish wonder is not only a response to spiritual and intellectual drama of this order. It is more apparent in small acts that turn an ordinary gesture into a grasp for immortality. The best example of this kind of transformative moment manifests itself in a rigorous Talmudic discussion of blessings. Pay attention to the astonishment that undergirds the following Talmudic passage about this aspect of Jewish law:

> Rabbi Joshua ben Levi said: One who sees a friend after a lapse of thirty days says: "Blessed is God who has kept us alive and preserved us and brought us to this season." If after a lapse of twelve months, he says: "Blessed is God who revives the dead." (Babylonian Talmud, *Berakhot* 58b)

The recitation of these two blessings is prompted by the pleasure and surprise that we feel in seeing people who, for one reason or another, have left our immediate orbit for a time. We are so delighted in the sudden renewal of their company that the blessing is a spontaneous articulation of both joy and wonder, particularly if a year has lapsed. In the pretechnological age in which this statement was written (this passage was probably redacted in the first centuries of the Common Era), not seeing a friend might signal that the friend is no longer alive. Our joy is more than a social nicety; it represents genuine happiness that time has preserved relationships of special importance to us.

In this instance, it is more than just pleasure that the visit arouses; it may be actual surprise, as is reflected in the astonishing choice of the blessing's words: "Blessed is God who revives the dead." The individual in question was not dead but was as if dead to the friend because of the lost contact; there can be little debate that revival of the dead is nothing less than a wondrous experience. A *tosafot* (a medieval Rabbinic commentary on the Talmud that appears side by side with the Talmudic text) observes that the blessing is only recited if the person we are seeing after a lengthy interval is actually someone we like. No blessing is to be said over those whose sudden appearance is either a neutral or a negative experience for us. In other words, no feeling of joy and wonder, no blessing.

This experience of joy extends far beyond the almost obvious happiness of seeing a companion. Wonder is the appropriate response to anything of surprise, whether it brings us joy or simply arouses our curiosity, as in the continuation of our Talmudic page:

> Our Sages taught: On seeing an elephant, an ape, or a long-tailed ape, one says: "Blessed is God who makes strange creatures." If one sees beautiful creatures and beautiful trees, one says: "Blessed is God who has such in God's world." (Babylonian Talmud, *Berakhot* 58b)

We can appreciate that seeing animals not normally in our human ambit would create a slight tremor, a "come and see this" sort of excitement that is shared with others. The author of an early medieval work of Jewish self-improvement, Bahya ibn Pakuda, writes of the animal world:

> Wisdom is manifest in the smallest creatures as in the largest. The force of wisdom displayed in the creation of the elephant, in its great body size, is no more marvelous than the force of wisdom displayed in the creation of the ant in its minuteness.[12]

This sentiment of wonder was shared by a later rabbi and outstanding Talmudic scholar, Rabbi Abraham Isaiah Karelitz (1878–1953), who also used his self-improvement manual to comment on the mystery of the elephant that ties into our ongoing conversation about habit, boredom, and personal responsibility:

> The familiarity of habit numbs the sense of wonder of the soul, [a capability] which befits every living creature by virtue of its being active. In contrast to this, the soul does feel wonder from special species which are not frequently seen, such as when a person sees an elephant or a monkey.[13]

Making a blessing over these fantastic creatures demonstrates that wonder in Jewish terms is not something about which we are secretive. Real wonder is shared wonder, over things large and small. Today, however, the wonder of elephants and monkeys, enticing and unusual things to see in medieval Baghdad or the Eastern Europe of the late twentieth century, has itself become habit for us as regular zoo visitors and travelers. There almost seems to be little that we have not seen, either personally or through the lens of someone else's camera in *National Geographic*. Reciting blessings helps us thank God but also helps us verbalize the experience, thereby making it richer and deeper for ourselves and as we share it with others.

To us, seeing an elephant or a monkey or watching an ant up close may feel like a hackneyed experience when, in reality, these creatures should present an enduring experience of wonder that always merits a blessing. If the grandeur of an elephant or the playfulness of a monkey does not move us, it is not the animal that must change, but the animal viewer.

The same piece of Talmud that we read above tells us that we must say blessings over earthquakes. Although they are a force of destruction, their very power shakes us and reminds us that we are not in control of the natural world. Danger is thrilling even in a religious context, but not in the sense of registering the absurd, foolish, or life-threatening. According to the Talmud, the rumbling of the earthquake is God speaking through nature. The blessing is a way that we tell God we are listening. "When the Holy One, blessed be God, calls to mind God's children, who are plunged in suffering among the nations of the world, God lets fall two tears into the ocean, and the sound is heard from one end of the world to the other and that is the rumbling" (Babylonian Talmud, *Berakhot* 59a). The earthquake in this poetic musing is caused by God's tears hitting the ocean on account of Jewish suffering. For that, we must take a moment and bear witness. And in articulating the blessing in this instance, we are also creating greater attachment to our surroundings and those responsible for them, in Fuller's words:

> Wonder entices us to consider the reality of the unseen, the existence of a more general order of existence from which this world

derives its meaning and purpose. It is thus only to be expected that wonder also entices us to believe that our supreme goal lies in harmoniously adjusting ourselves thereto. Wonder, it would seem, is one of the principal sources of humanity's spiritual impulse.[14]

If the connection between wonder and blessings has not been sufficiently spelled out, perhaps an illustration of the very act will provide the best resource for understanding.

Rabbi Joseph Soloveitchik, who has been cited before in these pages, shares with us his own personal and profound experience of blessing nature and becomes, in so doing, a teacher of wonder:

> I remember how enthused I was the first time I saw the Baltic Sea. I was born in Russia and never saw a major body of water in my youth.... I remember that the water was blue, deeply blue. From afar it looked like a blue forest. It resembled the aboriginal forests near Pruzhana, where I was born. When I came close and realized it was the Baltic Sea, I was overwhelmed by its beauty. Spontaneously, I began to recite the Psalm, "Bless the Lord, O my soul." I did not plan to do this. Yet the words flowed from my lips.... "There is the sea, vast and wide." It was a religious reaction to viewing the majesty of God's creation. When I recited the blessing upon seeing the sea, I did so with emotion and deep feeling. I deeply experienced the words of the benediction: "Blessed be He who wrought creation." Not all the blessings that I recite are said with such concentration. It was more than simply a blessing; it was an encounter with the Creator. I felt that the Shekhinah [Divine Presence] was hidden in the darkness and vastness of the sea. The experience welled out of me.[15]

This recollection brings us into a powerful spiritual moment that is profoundly personal. We are experiencing the Baltic Sea ... the depth of its color and its expansiveness through the eyes of Rabbi Soloveitchik, although he himself is recounting it decades later. He reminds us that we may not have these moments often, that our blessings do not always carry the same weight or tenderness, but that when they do, they become unforgettable pieces in the complex tapestry that is our spiritual life.

He also reminds us that such reactions to nature may be inherently felt, but they also need to be taught. Rabbi Soloveitchik believed that "it is up to ... the teacher to open up the emotional world of Judaism to the students."[16] Stated differently, we need teachers who experience wonder who can share that experience of wonder. A teacher who feels nurtured by and connected to his or her surroundings can give us the words and the intensity, even the very permission, to stop and smell the roses.

Speaking of roses, they too require a blessing. A fragrant smell, like flowers or spices, must be acknowledged as part of the miraculous sensual world in which we live. But the Talmud and the Rabbinic commentaries that follow it observe that not all smells are alike, even good smells. If a good smell is emitted from the incense of idolaters, it is not to be blessed. The experience of wonder is not disconnected from our ideological sensitivities or our sensitivities in general, as in the Talmudic recommendation that we not make a blessing over incense that is used in a funeral service, presumably because our wonder at the smell is dampened by the purpose of the smell in the first place.[17] If the smell is a perfume, a deodorant, or an air freshener that is used to mask a bad odor, then it, too, does not require a blessing precisely because its wafting aroma is there not as a cause of astonishment but rather as a means to avoid disappointment when in too close contact with an overpoweringly bad smell.

Spicing It Up

The Jewish law that perhaps best communicates how blessings recited habitually are connected with wonder, is this: "If one enters a spice dealer's shop and smells the fragrance, even though he [the spice dealer] sits the whole day, he only makes one blessing, but if he is constantly going in and out, he makes a blessing each time he enters" (Babylonian

Talmud, *Berakhot* 53a). This case brings us into the sights and smells of a Middle Eastern market. We immediately visualize an old man in front of gigantic burlap spice sacks whose sides are rolled down to reveal rich ochre shades of mustard and the orange of lentils and the smells of cardamom and rose water. If we enter the spice stall ourselves as customers, then we make a blessing over the rich aromas. According to one commentator, this blessing should only be recited if we intend to take in the smell of the spices, in other words, if the smell is something that makes us feel wonderful. If we do not like the smell of spices and are holding our noses so that we can buy just enough cumin for an Indian recipe, then forget the blessing.[18]

Our spice seller, who is sitting on a low stool and holding a glass of tea tightly, is in close contact with powerful odors all day and may even lose sensitivity to the smell. He may fail to notice the very strong smells that surround him, much like we fail to smell our own perfume, the mold in a basement, or the onions in a salad if exposed to them for many hours. The spice seller who sits in his stall all day makes one blessing, but if the same spice seller is negotiating with vendors and walking into multiple stalls, his nose reflects the wonder of each encounter, even though selling spices is his livelihood. There is a nuance to the smell of a new spice shop that his olfactory sense must be particularly attuned to in his profession. Although our old spice seller deals with smells all day, each time he encounters a smell anew, even minute variations of a smell, he notes them and thanks God for them.

The powerful sense of contextual and situational awareness induced by the making of blessings is also an antidote against boredom, where everything feels used and overly familiar. Every act of astonishment is a way of fighting tedium. Blessings are a religious pause and reflection of this awareness through prayer. The blessings we make on everything from an orange to the sight of a beautiful tree, thunder and the presence of a king, tell us that nothing escapes our attention in the sensual and intellectual realms of existence.

The Talmud recommends the recitation of one hundred blessings each day, slowing us down to create multiple moments of wonder. The nuances emerge in the change of language from one species to another, from one sensual experience to another. Some of these experiences are immensely visual, like the blessing upon seeing the Mediterranean Sea or seeing lightning before our eyes. Others have less to do with the way nature appears and more to do with attuning ourselves to the calendar and the passage of time. There is a blessing that we make only once a year on blossoming fruit trees in the Hebrew month of Nisan (during the same spring month as Passover). The first blossoming of a tree is easy to miss if we do not make a mental note of an actual obligation to create the moment and make much of one of nature's gifts. Our tradition continually tells us that one way to combat boredom is to produce blessings, to enhance the natural mystery and transcendence of the world by taking enough time to notice it.

Wonder and the Human Condition

Wonder, in the two Jewish examples we have explored in this chapter, is either an earth-shattering discovery that changes the religious world or a prosaic, transitory experience of marking a sensual moment and offering God a little credit for it. The two extremes magnify the question of whether wonder is a response of astonishment to a situation or whether it is something more, an approach to life perhaps. In the Abraham narrative, wonder is a dogged persistence inspired by curiosity that yields a radical and original conclusion. Blessings are small acts of marvel that embody a particular attitude about the world; it is a blessed place, and everything is a gift. Would blessings uttered by a person who is bored communicate that same attitude? Would a special discovery of enormous consequences be made by a scientist who did not marvel at the universe?

Heschel's Wonder

To understand the importance of wonder as a religious mindset, we turn to another great Jewish thinker of the past century, Abraham Joshua Heschel. Heschel was a majestic writer whose words have a buoyant, radiant quality to them. His writing about wonder is in itself wondrous.

He questions the nature of wonder, particularly from a spiritual viewpoint. All wonder is not the same. His term for religious wonder is *radical amazement*. Religious wonder is not only different qualitatively from scientific wonder; it feels greater than surprise. It is an attitude more than a temporal state or a response:

> Wonder or radical amazement is the chief characteristic of the religious man's attitude toward history and nature.... To find an approximate cause of a phenomenon is no answer to his ultimate wonder. He knows that there are laws that regulate the course of natural processes; he is aware of the regularity and pattern of things. However, such knowledge fails to mitigate his sense of perpetual surprise at the fact there are facts at all. Looking at the world he would say, "This is the Lord's doing; it is marvelous in our eyes."[19]

Even recognizing the way that the world operates will not diminish wonder but enhance it for the religious individual. Heschel continues to say that wonder can and often is the "feeling of a philosopher." The act of wonder stimulated philosophers to philosophize in the first place. They stood before that which they did not understand, be it matter, beauty, truth, or justice, and began to question and explore the component parts of whatever they put under scrutiny. Wonder, Heschel believed, was the prelude to knowledge. And yet, wonder ceases to exist, Heschel argued, "once the cause of a phenomenon is explained."[20]

Curiosity for a scientist or philosopher is not a perpetual state of wonder in the face of the unknown; it is a temporary mental condition that germinates into information, knowledge, or answers. On this philosophical or scientific level, wonder is problematic as a spiritual mechanism because once the mystery has been solved, it would seem that wonder instantly dissipates. For this reason, Heschel distinguished between philosophical wonder and spiritual wonder:

> But does the worth of wonder merely consist in its being a stimulant to the acquisition of knowledge? Is wonder the same

as curiosity? To the prophets, wonder is a form of thinking. It is not the beginning of knowledge but an act that goes beyond knowledge; it does not come to an end when knowledge is acquired; it is an attitude that never ceases. There is no answer in the world to man's radical amazement.[21]

Thus, wonder and curiosity are not the same because curiosity is not sustained when a problem is solved, whereas wonder as a way in which to approach the world, an attitude to inhabit in the face of all things, never departs. As Heschel says later in the same essay, "What fills us with radical amazement is not the relation in which everything is embedded but the fact that even the minimum of perception is a maximum of enigma."[22] It is a wonder that we *can* wonder, and this seems to be a distinctly human capacity that distinguishes us from other species. The rabbi and scholar Louis Jacobs, in exploring Heschel's language here, observes, "Man thinks, and he imagines that by thinking adequately about the world he can offer a full explanation of it. But he has left out the sheer marvel that man is able to think so profoundly. Our thought itself, our capacity to explain everything is without any explanation. It belongs to the wonder of existence."[23]

How is it that we think at all? This gift is itself an act of wonder, the "minimum of perception" that is a "maximum of enigma." Radical amazement rather than scientific inquiry keeps us filled with wonder all the time, unlike a magic trick that seems remarkable until we know how it is done. Heschel's amazement is the magic of our capacity to exist and think at all; it is not a limited curiosity at the way something works that can be unraveled and articulated.

We can hear wonder in the words of the psalmist: "I praise You, for I am awesomely, wondrously made; Your work is wonderful; I know it very well" (Psalm 139:14). The psalmist is conscious of an awe that overtakes him when he looks at his own body and the way that he is made. His realization that he is "marvelously made" spills over into all areas, and he is profoundly aware that all of God's worlds are stamped with the same wonder. Astonishment in this verse does not begin with that which is least known to us; it begins when we look at ourselves and expands to encompass all parts of the created world.

Boredom and Free Time

Poet, essayist, and naturalist Diane Ackerman, author of *A Natural History of the Senses*, talks about how much excitement we need to keep our senses active and make sure that boredom does not hijack us:

> Our senses also crave novelty. Any change alerts them, and they send a signal to the brain. If there's no change, no novelty, they doze and register little or nothing. The sweetest pleasure loses its thrill if it continues too long. A constant state—even of excitement—in time becomes tedious, fades into the background, because our senses have evolved to report changes, what's new, something startling that has to be appraised: a morsel to eat, a sudden danger. The body takes stock of the world like an acute and observant general moving through a complex battleground, looking for patterns and stratagems.... There is that unique moment when one confronts something new and astonishment begins. Whatever it is, it looms brightly, its edges sharp, its details ravishing, in a hard clear light; just beholding it is a form of revelation, a new sensory litany.... Living on the senses requires an easily triggered sense of marvel, a little extra energy, and most people are lazy about life. Life is something that happens to them while they wait for death.[24]

The edginess, clarity, and sharpness Ackerman describes are a view of life with a wide-angled lens; there is vibrancy and vitality to it. In the absence of astonishment, Ackerman arrives at a maudlin conclusion: life is just something that happens while waiting for death.

Reinventing Leisure Time

Perhaps in order to generate wonder, we need to think harder about how we spend our free time. Rabbi Norman Lamm, the former president of Yeshiva University, in writing on the ethics of leisure, observes that leisure refers not only to the use of time in a specific way but also to the nature of the activity. He compares the drudgery of carrying a load up many flights of stairs, which seems tedious and laborious, to the same level of exertion in a gym, which may seem exhilarating because of the way that we think of it. Lamm writes:

> Leisure is a game activity in the highest sense. We place a person in a new environment, in new conditions, allow him to bring out unsuspected skills that were heretofore latent in him, to express himself in new ways, whether of esthetics or athletics or any other way to which he is unaccustomed during the week.[25]

The sense of leisure as skill development in an area that is not generally employed during a workday is a very different way of regarding leisure from the sense of simple relaxation. Leisure is not doing nothing. There is something refreshing about the novelty offered in this definition. After all, if we regard leisure as doing nothing, then it is easy to see why leisure would itself become boring. Much more exciting, however, is the notion that my body and mind are championing new skills or talents. I discover abilities in myself that were either dormant or atrophied.

Lamm then takes this definition and adds a welcome Jewish spin to it by introducing the Hebrew term for "leisure," *nofesh*, which is related to the term for "soul," which is *nefesh*:

> *Nofesh* is more than self-*discovery*; it is the use of leisure for self-*transformation*.... Instead of activity for the purpose of self-*expression*, it may require a certain kind of personal, inner silence in which you make yourself available for a higher *impression*. It is the incorporation of the transcendent rather than the articulation of the immanent. You try to respond to something that comes from without, from above. *Nofesh* means not to fulfill yourself but to go outside yourself, to rise beyond yourself; not to *discover* your identity, but rather to *create* a new and better identity. *Nofesh* requires of us that we take our creative talents, which during the week are applied to impersonal nature or

unengaged society, and now turn them inwards and create a new, real self. This is the inner and deeper meaning of *menuhah*: it is *re-creation*, not relaxation.[26]

Lamm spends less time on the wordplay and more on the nuance of the way we regard leisure. Ideally, in Jewish terms, while leisure is a time to uncover talents previously hidden, the way Winston Churchill discovered the power of a blank canvas at age forty, it is also and primarily a time for self-reflection that leads to seeking higher, transcendent ground. What is relaxing about *nofesh* is not that we are responding to external drives, challenges, or stimuli, like running a marathon or catching a fish, but that we spend quiet time with ourselves understanding and perhaps experiencing harmony with the world. That, in itself, becomes a source of deep relaxation. The old notion of rest and relaxation gives way to the active creation of identity, thickening our emotional, spiritual, and intellectual drives in ways that are uniquely self-determined.

For many people, hobbies, like work, are other venues to demonstrate competence or competitiveness. Far from feeling relaxed, these hobbies can become their own source of stress. Free time is not about leisure but about proving excellence and driving their bodies or minds hard, pushing to an extreme to get a better outcome. Fishing, a potentially quiet and contemplative sport that may give the mind plenty of blank space to reflect, can become a source of frustration when there is no fish on the end of the line by the end of the day. After all, there is an objective to the sport, and silence and communion with nature are only happy by-products for some. A relative who was enormously frustrated that on his vacation he failed to catch a single fish was told by a wise fisherman on the shore, "Son, it's called fishing, not catching."

While it is true that these examples of "leisure ambition" can be filled with self-discovery about our own abilities, it can also drive us mad in the process. It can accomplish the very opposite of what true respite seeks to provide: freedom from external pressures to explore deeper meaning and feel at peace with yourself and your surroundings. It is here that the wordplay is critical. *Nofesh* and *nefesh* are rooted in the same Hebrew word, indicating that true rest is an awakening of the soul. It is a time when distinctive aspects of self are allowed time for expression and space for articulation.

Nofesh, with its emphasis on transcendence, implies up-time, literally. In the psychological and spiritual definitions of leisure offered here, leisure by its essential nature cannot be determined by cultural expectations of relaxation. It must reflect our own unique needs, since often it represents our only realistic opportunity to shape time. Joseph Pieper, a German Catholic philosopher, wrote about the connection of leisure and personal identity in his book, *Leisure: The Basis of Culture*:

> Leisure is possible only on the premise that man consents to his own true nature, and abides in concord with the meaning of the universe.... Leisure draws its vitality from affirmation. It is not the same as non-activity.[27]

Jewish Wonder

Arnold Posy (1892–1986) was a Yiddish essayist who left White Russia for London as a child and then immigrated to the United States in 1920. Unlike many of his generation, he remained traditional and struggled with the changes in religious observance of his generation. His interest in Hasidut and mysticism offered him an outlook on the world that inclined to wonder, and he wrote an article called "Belief in Judaism in a Generation of Disbelief" to question those who had relinquished faith. The key to faith, for Posy, was recapturing wonder:

> So we see and we feel with all our senses the sheer wonder of the world, the vast miracle and miracles of Nature. At the same time we become aware of the vast, concealed spiritual powers of man. And it all confronts us with riddles that we cannot possibly solve. They arouse a sense of awe and spiritual exaltation in us.[28]

Posy quotes a student of the Baal Shem Tov, one of the great Hasidic masters, who tries to fathom the wonder of wonder:

"Look up to the heaven and count the stars," said one of the Baal Shem's disciples. "Man can see God's sublimity most when he looks up to heaven and sees the course of the stars and the wonderful lights they give. That is how man can fill himself with the wonder of God.... How much greater is the wonder when man considers himself and comes to realize the wonder of the Divine Spirit that was put into him."[29]

The wonder of wonder is that when we are awed by the vastness of what is outside of us, the stars, the ocean, the mountains, we become filled with wonder at the divinity that is inside us. This transformative process can take place in any number of settings, and often the ones least predictable yield the greatest results.

The Wonder of Seeing

A professor of art, James Elkins wrote a book titled *Pictures and Tears* to document the phenomenon of those who cried in front of paintings. He asks why and how this happens and concludes with the observation that given the nature of art, it really should happen more often. There can be so much wonder contained in a moment perfectly painted on canvas that we weep for the perfection, the emotion, the absolute beauty. Elkins suggests that perhaps those of us who are dry-eyed in art museums need to wonder about our lack of wonder. Elkins ruminates:

> The twentieth century has gotten us out of the habit. Our museums and universities breed people with a cool demeanor. Weeping doesn't fit the ironic tone of postmodernism. There is a list of other reasons, but the best single answer, if I had to choose just one, is that it's comforting to think that paintings require only domesticated, predictable emotions. Everyone knows more intimate encounters might be possible.[30]

To help take us out of our twentieth-century tearless prison, Elkins asked for testimonies of those living today who have cried in front of paintings.

He shares them in the appendix to his book, and I will share with you his absolute favorite:

> Hello,
>
> I cried in a museum in front of a Gauguin painting—because somehow he had managed to paint a transparent pink dress. I could almost see the dress wafting in the breeze.
>
> I cried at the Louvre in front of Victory. She had no arms, but she was so tall.
>
> I cried (so hard I had to leave) in a little concert where a young man played solo cello Bach suites. It was in a weird little Methodist church and there were only about fifteen of us in the audience, the cellist alone on the stage. It was midday. I cried because (I guess) I was overcome with love. It was impossible for me to shake the sensation (mental, physical) that J. S. Bach was in the room with me, and I loved him.
>
> These three instances (and the others I am now recollecting) I think have something to do with loneliness … a kind of craving for the company of beauty. Others, I suppose, may say God.
>
> But this feels too simple a response.[31]

The sense of being overcome with love or harmony is an act of revelation. We stand before something we all recognize, but suddenly it means something else because we have stopped to really look, to listen with our eyes, and in this small act of attentiveness have achieved wonder. We stand in front of a painting and tears stream down our cheeks.

Mystic Wonder

This wonder of newness and majesty is captured marvelously by Rabbi Abraham Isaac Kook (1864–1935), the first Ashkenazi chief rabbi of Israel and a great mystic and poet, in his reflections on the nature of becoming:

> An epiphany enables you to sense creation not as something completed, but as constantly becoming, evolving, ascending.

This transports you from a place where there is nothing new to a place where there is nothing old, where everything renews itself, where heaven and earth rejoice as at the moment of Creation.[32]

Wonder transports you from a place where there is nothing new to a place where there is nothing old, where everything seems to shine and sing.

9 Boredom and Authenticity

> Boredom: the desire for desires.
>
> *Leo Tolstoy,* Anna Karenina

An Internet ad for the 2008 Ford Escape, a midsize SUV, tells the onlooker that the car is an escape from boredom. The campaign is called "Boredom Hurts—The 2008 Ford Escape Is the Cure." The car is more than a transportation vehicle. It is a cure for a pervasive societal illness. The ad introduces Colin Padden, a bored-looking college student sitting at the edge of a doctor's table in a hospital gown. He is being diagnosed. Colin writes a blog and fills empty time with little else. For evidence of his boredom, the viewer is directed to a computer with the following words on the screen: "A boredom outbreak is sweeping across the nation." The screen advertises that it is gathering evidence of boredom from personal confessionals, cries for help, and boredom-inspired stunts. If you suffer boredom, you can submit your evidence. Why is Colin gathering evidence? He explains that on his blog:

> At the end of the 19th century, a new disease began to take root ... And I believe it started right here in my own back-yard. My name is Colin Padden, and I'm a doctoral candidate in Environmental Engineering at Oregon A&M University. For a while, my life seemed perfect—great job, loving live-in girlfriend (hi, Amy!), and too many friends to count. I was

happy ... I was content ... I missed all the warning signs. Last
year, after giving an adjunct lecture, I began feeling excep-
tionally lifeless and rundown. As the days wore on, the
symptoms only got worse. Lifelessness gave way to listlessness, listlessness to indifference, indifference to apathy, and
apathy circled lazily around to give way to lifelessness again.
Every aspect of my life was affected—every aspect (much to
Amy's dismay) ... Something had to be done. I consulted
with everyone I could find—faculty, doctors, clergy, family—
I was getting nowhere. Finally, a chance encounter with an
"alternative healer" started me down my current road to
recovery ... I was told I suffered from the "Boring Bug"—a
devastating disorder to which the cure remains unknown. I
had heard of this disease before—always chalking it up as
merely myth, an urban (if not rural) legend. But my gut was
now telling me otherwise. What exactly is the "Boring Bug"?
What are the causes? What is the relief? What is the truth
about ... boredom? Being of a scientific mind, I am determined to find physical evidence and proof that an Epidemic
of Boredom has indeed returned, and runs rampant around
this great country of ours. I started this site to share my ail-
ment and story with you, and hope others will come forward
with cases of Boredom in their own lives. If we share our stories, we can work to find a cure.[1]

Our bored college student suddenly offers a brief history of boredom,
how it influences society, and how it is affecting him personally. Not
really what we would expect from a car ad.

Colin is not only in need of wheels; he is really a scientist, you
see, who wants to take apart the disease through research. Evidence.
Testimonies. Stories. This fabricated blog offers us a bizarre way to
view boredom—as part of a personal narrative leading us to greater
purchasing power. You still may not be able to afford the car, however, which is a shame, since it eliminates the problem of boredom
permanently.

An Authentic Self

Colin longs, we all long, for a return to what felt like a more authentic self. The psychologist Erich Fromm argues that boredom is a uniquely human problem that has the power to distance us from the authentic self we crave: "Man is the only animal that can be bored, that can be discontented, that can feel evicted from paradise."[2] Boredom does not affect any other species but human beings. We simply cannot imagine a cow, for instance, standing in a field on all fours and, in between chewing, spurting out, "I can't stand eating grass anymore. I'm bored, and I'm tired of this field," even though a bovine existence seems terribly tedious to us. An old *New Yorker* cartoon positions a chicken next to his feathered friend, telling him in confidence, "I don't want to be a chicken anymore." It seems absurd. Yet questioning our essence is a uniquely human preoccupation. So, too, is boredom a human social construction. Animals do not question their existence; therefore, animals cannot be bored by it.

The Talmud was intrigued by this very notion, and while generally humans are viewed as superior to other animals from the first chapter of Genesis onward, humans fight dangers that other animals never encounter that remove them from their ultimate purpose:

> Rabbi Simon the son of Eleazar said, "All my days I have not seen a deer blush, a lion suffer, or a fox feel compassion, and they sustain themselves without pain, even though they were created only for my service. Yet, I was created to serve my Master—while they were only created to serve me—allow me to serve my Master without pain. (Babylonian Talmud, *Kiddushin* 71b)

Rabbi Simon observed the natural world and came to a surprising question. Why is it that we are not more like animals, who do not feel human emotions but who also do not question the essential purpose of their existence? They serve humans without doubt, rebellion, ingratitude, or attitude, and yet we, who are imbued with a range of human emotion, suffer confusion and do doubt ourselves and question God.

Why? Because to be human is to question authority, to debate purposefulness, and also to suffer in its absence. The Talmud emphasizes unquestioning service in this passage, either animal service to humans or human service to God. Service is not a simple formula for a life occupation in our swath of Talmud. It is something that humans fight and resist and define themselves against. If not, Rabbi Simon would never have juxtaposed the way that animals respond to their calling and the way that humans resist theirs. But when we look closer at the notion of service as a response to boredom, we discover something interesting about personal identity. We often find ourselves, our purpose, and our sense of meaning precisely in the act of losing ourselves.

If boredom is understood as a constant personal review of unchanging options, it becomes a narcissistic preoccupation where we anticipate and predict actions and reactions. Serving others not only adds fullness to our lives, but it also offers the unpredictability that is always anticipated when dealing with others who do not share our cultural or emotional assumptions about human behavior and the world. Losing ourselves means letting go of rigid self-understanding in favor of greater receptivity. It may also imply disciplining ourselves to achieve what we feel is morally right and good in a scheme grander than one we could create ourselves. We lose ourselves to others and also to ideas and may, in the process, discover more about our inner workings than we knew before.

A Desire for Desire

If we are really living in a time of happiness and abundance, then why do so many suffer Anna Karenina's desire for desire? Why does the religious life no longer fill that empty emotional and spiritual vacuum? Rabbi Jonathan Sacks, chief rabbi of the United Hebrew Congregation of the British Commonwealth and author, shares his thoughts on the problem:

> Why, if things are so good, are they so bad? The shortest, simplest answer is that we have lost our way. We have focused on the how but not the why. In achieving material abundance we have begun to lose our moral and spiritual bearings. In achiev-

ing technical mastery we have lost sight of the question—to what end?... Luckily, all that we have lost is recoverable.... The human spirit is unique in its capacity to count its own errors. What we damage, we can repair.[3]

Rabbi Sacks's words resonate. We often hear it said that materialism damages our moral and spiritual bearings. Why should it? If anything, material success should enable us to achieve more, give more, and be more of ourselves, rather than less. For many, financial enrichment does yield these benefits, but all too often having more than we need dampens our hunger and drive. It takes away the need to need. Philosopher Sean Desmond Healy makes this very observation:

> So many have achieved so much so fast that dreams of success have been overtaken by the reality and have lost their strength as sources of collective meaning binding society together. This is especially true of so many of the young, who come into a world of apparently almost infinite and easy plenty, but who experience it as in some indefinable way inadequate. They seem to be seeking without even knowing what they are looking for, the missing center of gravity that would give weight to their existence, only to find, or to sense, that their culture provides none.[4]

Through all the preparatory stages of our education, early work experience, and relationships, we begin a difficult process of differentiation. Who am I? What kind of friendships sustain me? What are my interests? What kind of lifestyle am I aiming for as an adult? And yet, if we always ask these questions of ourselves, we can become too self-absorbed.

Professor and author Richard Winter, in his book *Still Bored in a Culture of Entertainment*, contends that narcissism makes us bored in the first place. Pursuing ways to entertain and distract ourselves will never heal us of boredom because when we spend too much time with ourselves, preening and grooming, in thought and self-judgment, in search of amusement, we also get bored of ourselves.

We are called not only to enjoy the world of God's creation but also to love our neighbors as we love ourselves. Throughout the Bible we find a strong emphasis on serving others. One of the reasons why boredom has become so much more common is because we have become too preoccupied with looking after ourselves, making sure our needs are met and, to put it bluntly, we have become too selfish.[5]

If you asked a bored person if he or she is selfish, the answer would probably be a resounding "No." Yet, if we define selfishness as an excessive or exclusive concern for our own benefits or pleasures without regard for others, we begin to see the seeds of boredom and discontent. When people describe themselves as bored, what they may be saying is that they can think of nothing interesting to do to entertain *themselves*.

They do not mean that they have exhausted all of the possible ways that they could be helping others. They do not mean that they have the "inner resources" to entertain themselves. They also do not mean that they intend to spend time thinking about themselves or contemplating the universe at large. Boredom, at its most dangerous, gets in the way of reaching the authentic self because it is a state of inactivity blamed on external forces. Healy regards boredom as a souped-up lack of interiority. This state, he believes, is intensifying: "Hyperboredom is on the rise because of man's failure to understand and respect the real nature of the self."[6]

Boredom and *Teshuva*

Teshuva in English means "return" but is used in religious parlance to indicate repentance. Repentance in the Jewish tradition is regarded not as change but as a return to God and a return to our most authentic selves. The steps of repentance are numerous and include recognition of sin, confession, and commitment not to err again. In any process of forgiveness that is beneath surface and clichéd resolution lies an acknowledgment of personal identity in its most profound sense. To return to self must involve a priori, a knowledge of the authentic self to which one can return. It is helpful in considering any profound personal changes to hold up a visual model in our minds of the self we like best and ask critical questions of this shadow self:

- What kind of behaviors bring out the best in me?
- What kind of settings and contexts bring out the best in me?
- Which people bring out the best in me? Around whom do I like myself best?

This process of repentance is not becoming an unrecognizable self but *returning* to a portrait of self that we already know and love but seems distant from us in the here and now.

The next step in the process of repentance is to determine the distance between that beloved sense of self and the self we occupy now and to chart the course of change:

- What will it take to become that self?
- What will it then take to sustain that self?
- How will I maintain that self when I am not in a setting that brings out that best self?

These questions are not meant to portray a glib, easy process, with easy metrics and a map. Fill out the forms and the fun begins. Simply asking the right questions does not make the act of repentance happen. It is complex and tortuous for many, with many setbacks and errors of judgment. *Teshuva* involves decisions; identity is always a matter of choice. We make choices about who we ultimately want to be. But at times, it does not always feel like we have ultimate control. There are all kinds of mitigating circumstances and people who seem to stand in the way. And the biggest obstacle is self-determination.

Maimonides interrupts his "Laws of Repentance" midstream to discuss free will. Without a belief that we are ultimately in charge of our destinies, we would never be able to change. We would go through the motions that Maimonides discusses in his first four chapters without the real and enduring belief that it will make any difference. In fact, Maimonides writes that anyone has the capacity to be as righteous as Moses, a startling objective, and one that may have never crossed our minds.

Recognizing the difficulty of achieving our real and authentic selves, *Pirkei Avot* (Ethics of the Fathers) 4:18 recommends that we exile ourselves to learn Torah. Maimonides mentions that we exile ourselves to repent.[7] Both statements reflect the real difficulty of change in a familiar setting, since others often do not allow us to change. They do not make room for our new selves because they believe that they really know us as we truly are. Alternatively, we do not let ourselves change because of the expectations of others. They want or even need us to be a particular person, and we shape ourselves accordingly. When we exile ourselves, we make decisions to go to an alternate landscape, both real and emotional, which will allow us the thrilling capacity to be the shapers of our identities, no holds barred.

Teshuva and Boredom

What does repentance have to do with boredom? We do not generally think of boredom as a sin that requires penitence or that boredom will have met its match through personal transformation. We believe that we require external stimulation so that boredom will disappear. This mistaken notion that boredom lies outside the self and that its solution also lies outside the self is the first and most critical error we make when analyzing the pervasive influence of boredom. To be bored within religious literature, as has been demonstrated in the previous chapters, is to show disregard for our surroundings, a casual dismissal of all that is lofty, holy, and beautiful with neglect, a simple wash of sarcasm, or effortless disdain. *Teshuva* cannot possibly heal all that.

Or can it? In *The Lights of Penitence*, Rabbi Abraham Isaac Kook writes about anomie as a very personal battle of forces within each individual that lays claim to his or her soul. He offers a startling interpretation of a Talmudic passage (Babylonian Talmud, *Yoma* 86a) on repentance in his masterwork, *The Lights of Penitence*. The passage states that when I repent, the world repents with me. How can it be that when

I repent the world repents with me? Surely I am not self-centered enough to believe that the world merely mimics my behavior and, in effect, orbits around me. Rabbi Kook analyzes this Talmudic statement and believes that when we change, the world looks different *to us*. When we repent, we look at the world with more optimism and hope. We redeem the world not because it has changed, but because *we* have changed.[8]

We also redeem the world when we repent because we feel ourselves to be wholly part of it; when we change, the world cannot help but change, because we are responsible for it. And yet, the world can only change when we take the first step in the dark corners of our own minds and behaviors:

> Penitence is inspired by the yearning of all existence to be better, purer, more vigorous and on a higher plane than it is. Within this yearning is a hidden life-force for overcoming every factor that limits and weakens existence.[9]

Rabbi Kook believes that the community and its dictates are an essential moral, spiritual, and emotional anchor for the individual. When a person feels distant from this anchoring body, he or she loses grounding and begins to doubt the self and the striving for higher objectives. For Rabbi Kook, the cost is also intellectual, since a comprehension of the world should be integrally connected to a refined sense of obligation and concern for humanity at large:

> How wrongdoing dulls the intelligence, both the intelligence of the individual and the intelligence of society, of a generation and of an epoch! The divine word reaches a person from all of its sources, from the Torah, from religious faith, from ancestral customs, from social mores, from his inner sense of equity—all these are channeled from the core reality in the spiritual order and its fullness, in the laws of heaven and earth, and their most basic essence. When degeneration leads him to embrace an outlook on life that negates his higher vision, then he becomes

prey to the dark side within him, to his weaker self. The result is that he cannot muster the strength to hold on to the orderly structure of life as it makes its claims on him … all things have changed…. The operative light of the mind … this light has darkened. And this light is the secret of life itself, the vitality in which the soul finds its sustenance.[10]

Rabbi Kook believes that the order and structure that give meaning and anchor an individual are pushed aside by wrongdoing. The basic ontological principles that guide life are turned upside down, and what remains is an outlook that minimizes human dignity and weakens the control that human beings must exert in this life to have their inner light shine and make them feel whole and significant.

The intellect can actually get in the way of this process of signification because many intelligent people think themselves above God and community. They have no need for this anchoring; that is something that only those less gifted need. Surprisingly, we do associate boredom with intelligence when it manifests itself as a certain kind of patronizing distance, a condescending superiority that spills over into dismissiveness. To see how boredom influences change within the Jewish tradition, we turn to the marvel of the Jewish story.

"The Clever Man and the Simpleton": A Cautionary Tale

Between 1806 and 1810, the Hasidic master Rabbi Nachman of Breslov, Ukraine, told thirteen tales to his disciples that have been told and retold ever since.[11] These tales are simple in their plotline but profoundly sophisticated in their implicit messaging. Although his tales deal with particular themes, those of simplicity and simple faith are recurring motifs. The tale "The *Hakham* and the *Tam*" ("The Clever Man and the Simpleton") is one of the most intriguing of Rabbi Nachman's endearing stories, not least because it deals with boredom and authenticity. Some may recognize the names as two of the four sons of the Haggadah. This cannot be purely coincidental, but these epithets are turned on their head in this story, making us question the value of sophistication over simplicity.

In our tale, two wealthy men each had a son. One had a wise son and the other a simpleton. They grew up fast friends. The fathers both had a turn of fate and lost their affluence, forcing the boys to fend for themselves. The simple son learned to mend shoes. The clever son decided to put off work for travel, since he could not lower himself to learn a common trade. He traveled to many different countries, learned various skills, and became employed in various fields, tiring quickly of each and feeling himself superior to his work. He went to Spain and studied philosophy and medicine. His experience and intelligence set him apart from others: "Afterwards, the world began to seem like nothing in his eyes." He was above it all. But this caused him great distress: "And he traveled home. And he suffered greatly on the road, since he had no one to talk to because of his wisdom. And he did not find lodgings to his liking and he suffered greatly."

In the meantime, the simple son made shoes and found a wife. He was not a good shoemaker, simple as he was, and he got less for his shoes than other shoemakers did for theirs because his shoes always had defects. The simpleton, however, never saw the mistakes. He imagined that he was better than he truly was in all kinds of ways. "And he was only full of joy and gladness at all times." The simpleton was overjoyed to learn that his old, smart friend was coming back home and greeted him upon his arrival with a special blessing. The clever son was not interested in the blessing of this simpleton. "And the *hakham* stared at him. The entire world was nothing to him, all the more so such a man who seemed like a madman." The clever man suffered greatly back home. He could not find lodgings that were acceptable to his tastes and complained bitterly until the simpleton questioned him: "A wise and rich man like you, why are you always suffering? Look, I am joyous." And the simpleton gave him another blessing: "May the Lord bring you up to my level."

The clever man was insulted and retorted that it was possible, with madness or illness, for the clever man to become like the simpleton, God forbid, but what was impossible was for the simpleton to become as clever as the wise man. The simpleton said, "With the Lord, blessed be

God, everything is possible. And it is possible that in an instant I should attain your cleverness." The clever man just laughed.

As it turned out, the simpleton was very much loved for his joy. Through a series of strange events, the king sent out two letters calling for a wise man and a simpleton. The wise man did not believe that the king had really sent for him and doubted and doubted until he believed there was no king at all. The simpleton responded right away, and the king took to him and, over time, appointed him a government minister. The simpleton was a good politician because he was innocent and governed with truth and honesty. He did not have a beguiling nature and became even more loved for his innocence. He also learned about the world through his new authority and became more clever.

In the meantime, a series of unfortunate and self-initiated events placed the *hakham* in danger, and he was kidnapped by the devil. In their last confrontation, the simpleton said to the clever man, "You told me that you could reach my level easily, and that I could not reach yours. See, I have already reached yours, but you have not yet reached mine. And I see it is more difficult for you to reach my simplicity."

In these stories, the king is always the King of Kings: God. Our story is not so much about God as it is about the nature of living. The clever son thought so much of himself that he put himself above others and suffered as a result. Through his clever but convoluted logic, he even denied God's existence. One scholar reads this story as a condemnation of the Enlightenment and those who spread themselves beyond the ghetto walls, educated themselves, and believed they were advancing themselves, when they lost their very souls.[12]

Yet, this story, by its very nature, is open to many interpretations. It may also be a comment on cultures and not only on individuals. It is a tale of what happens when a culture becomes so sophisticated that it can find no relief in simple pleasures. It is a culture that becomes so cynical that it finds nothing worthy of thought or action. It begins to deny or undermine its very purpose and invites suffering. Even in its suffering, it regards itself as superior.

A Culture of Anomie

The sociologist Emile Durkheim (1858–1917) used a different word to describe this malaise: *anomie*, signifying moral and emotional detachment that weakened the bonds between people and society at large. Durkheim was concerned with the question at the heart of this book. When you take away religion and shared communal values in favor of strident individualism, what replaces it to ensure communal cohesion?

Religion has always provided a language of ritual and community, even when particular individuals struggled against its norms and conventions. In its absence, something must fill the vacuum. In 1897, Durkheim published his book *Suicide*, which discusses social integration, the way in which individuals cohere to society through limited affinities. He discovered that the rate of suicide among Catholics was less than among Protestants. He believed that this was due to a stronger social integration among Catholics; a more demanding communal structure was placed on individuals in the Catholic tradition, like a holding net, which created great safety, support, and comfort.

For Durkheim, anomie is social instability caused by an erosion of standards and values. Anomie is the alienation and purposelessness experienced by a person or a class as a result of a lack of standards, values, or ideals:

> A mind that questions everything, unless strong enough to bear the weight of its ignorance, risks questioning itself and being engulfed in doubt. If it cannot discover the claims to existence of the objects of its questioning—and it would be miraculous if it so soon succeeded in solving so many mysteries—it will deny them all reality, the mere formulation of the problem already implying an inclination to negative solutions. But in so doing it will become void of all positive content and, finding nothing which offers it resistance, will launch itself perforce into the emptiness of inner reverie.[13]

The void of positive content of which Durkheim speaks takes us directly to the clever son's dismissal of a profession. He questions the value of work and the lowering of himself to common purpose. He questions but is overloaded with his questions to the point of denying reality. In place of a healthy reality, emptiness sets in, corroding the fabric of his very existence. As a result, we do not feel sympathetic to the suffering of the clever son when he cannot find lodgings to his liking. Ironically, his pain feels simplistic and self-serving. We feel that he has brought about his own suffering. In contrast, the simple man is so simple that people laugh at his rose-colored glasses. He sees beauty where there are defects, promise where there is none, and innocence in place of craftiness. Although we cannot approve of his ill-made shoes and may be hesitant to buy a pair for ourselves, we admire his naiveté, his desire to redeem the ugly and see the world as better than it actually is.

And there is also the matter of the mental wager that the clever son makes with the simpleton. The clever man does not believe that a simpleton can ever become wise, although he does believe that a clever person can become simple. It seems, on face value, to be true. But as the story unfolds, Rabbi Nachman has us thinking counterintuitively. The simpleton gains enormous wisdom through life experience. He allows himself to be taught by joy. He becomes elevated in society by virtue of innocence and kindness, the kind of reward we wish for him in a less-than-perfect world where clever but cruel people so often succeed. The clever man, however, will never achieve simplicity because he both denies its utility and belittles its value. Many sophisticated people laud simple faith because they believe in the impossibility of achieving it for themselves.

As a story of boredom, Rabbi Nachman's tale is especially rich. The clever son seeks out excitement through travel and study. He refuses to give in to the pull of everyday ordinary life: finding a job, seeking a wife, living in community. The simple son never leaves home. He stays put and embraces a life of habituation that would seem entirely boring to the clever son. As the clever son adds up his life experiences, he begins to suffer because of the distance he sees between himself and others. This detachment, withdrawal, and judgment are typical behaviors describing boredom. Think of the bored student who withdraws to the last row of seats in a classroom, feels detached from the teacher's conversation, and judges the learning to be a waste of time, beneath him. Such is Rabbi Nachman's clever son.

In the end, this son is metaphorically kidnapped by the devil, in the clutches of a harsh and unforgiving master; his new life mirrors the self-initiated torment he willingly embraced during his lifetime. Rabbi Nachman also left his disciples and his future readers with a formidable challenge: to choose how we interpret purposeful living, to live accordingly, and to judge the quality of a life. We choose boredom; we can also choose innocence.

Growth through Conflict

Rabbi Nachman is not the only storyteller for this chapter. A popular leadership guru, Patrick Lencioni, writes fables that illustrate organizational problems, generally rooted in human behavior. His books have been used by everyone from corporate executives to the NFL to explore teamwork and the obstacles to cooperation. One of his fables is captured in the book *Death by Meeting*. When we think of boredom, virtually nothing compares in the extent of its tedium as the typical meeting. People posture and pontificate, repeat and reaffirm, reassert and rebuff. Like some complicated game, words fly through the air, but issues rarely get decided. In Lencioni's fable, a major corporate executive is about to lose his job in a merger. To hold on to his position requires a degree of charisma that he cannot muster. By chance, his secretary goes on maternity leave at this tenuous time and is temporarily replaced by a young man, the son of a friend, who is in film school and looking for a summer position. The young man attends and writes minutes for meetings, a job that sounds tortuous in the way that these meetings are described. Being thoughtful, ambitious, and also concerned about his father's friend, the CEO, he brazenly offers some advice to his boss.

Why is it, he contends, that a two-hour meeting is dull, while a two-hour movie might keep you on the edge of your seat? Most meetings and movies last about the same amount of time, and yet there is a deep chasm of interest that separates the two. After much deliberation, this upstart tells his boss that writing movies that are interesting is all about capturing and inviting conflict, the kind of tension that keeps people engaged and interested long beyond the typical attention span. Meetings are tedious because they do not allow for sufficient conflict and resolution. There may be very significant tensions in the group, both personal and professional differences of opinion, but meetings are so politely manicured or tightly controlled that these tensions are not allowed proper expression, a reason that meetings tend not to bring issues to their necessary resolution. For those of you who are curious, this advice is taken most seriously by our desperate CEO. His meetings become so engaging that not only does he keep his job, but he also is responsible for soaring stocks and his own promotion.

Lencioni's point is obvious and brilliant in its simplicity. Conflict makes meetings interesting. To extend it beyond the corporate metaphor, synagogue services are also approximately the length of a movie. Depending on the denomination, services may be a bit shorter or may be as long as a double feature. And yet it's a lot easier to convince the family to go to the movies than it is to go to the synagogue down the street. We don't expect synagogue services to be filled with conflict; many people go to have an oasis of decorum and meditation apart from their normal activities.

We do expect, however, that religion is not a sugar pill and that to be meaningful and interesting it must wrap itself around complex and difficult issues. Some of the most sophisticated writers on Judaism concur that Judaism is not for the faint-hearted. It is for those who are willing and able to invite conflict and tension into their lives as a means of personal growth. Read the first passage from Heschel and the second and third passages from Luzzatto to get a feel for how this conflict is manifest:

> To live means to walk perpetually on the edge of a precipice. The human predicament is a state of constant and irresolvable tension between mighty opposites. Piety and prudence, Truth and self-interest, are irreconcilable. Tension and conflict can no more be eliminated from thought than from life.[14]

> A person's nature exercises a strong downward pull upon him.... If he leaves himself in the hands of his downward-

pulling nature, there is no question that he will not succeed. As the Tanna [author of the Mishnah] says, "Be as fierce as a leopard, light as an eagle, swift as a deer and as strong as a lion to do the will of your Father in heaven" [*Pirkei Avot* (Ethics of the Fathers) 5:23]. Our Sages of blessed memory have numbered Torah and good deeds among those things which require self-fortification [Babylonian Talmud, *Berakhot* 32b].[15]

The man whose soul burns in the service of his Creator will surely not idle in the performance of His mitzvah, but his movements will be like the quick movements of a fire; he will not rest or be still until the deed has been completed. Furthermore, just as zeal can *result* from an inner burning so can it *create* one. That is, one who perceives a quickening of his outer movements in the performance of a mitzvah conditions himself to experience a flaming inner movement, through which longing and desire will continually grow. If, however, he is sluggish in the movement of his limbs, the movement of his spirit will die down and be extinguished. Experience testifies to this.... The man in whom this longing does not burn as it should would do well to bestir himself by force of will so that, as a result, this longing will spring up in his nature; for outer movements awaken inner ones. Unquestionably, a person has more control of his outer than his inner self, but if he makes use of what he can control, he will acquire, in consequence, even that which is not within the province of his control. For as a result of the willed quickening of his movements, there will arise in him an inner joy and a desire and a longing.... "After God they will go, who will roar like a lion" [Hosea 11:10].[16]

These paragraphs, little wrapped packages of meaning, all point to a tradition rich in movement and passion, tension and elevation. We see flames and revisit the lion's roar. According to Heschel, the Kotzker Rebbe believed powerfully in the insight of the individual: "God loves novelty," he said. Mere repetitiveness was contemptible. Individualism involves newness, creativity.[17]

Religion in these portraits is not staid and conventional; it is a means to inspire, to refresh, to express, and to articulate complication and tension.

Boredom, or What's in a Name?

According to *The Oxford English Dictionary*, the word *boredom* dates to the mid-nineteenth century. It is not a very old word linguistically. The word *interesting* appears in the English language at approximately the same time, give or take a decade or two. The American essayist Logan Pearsall Smith (1865–1946) made the original observation that *bore* and *interesting* first appeared in print about two years apart.

While the *OED* offers slightly greater spacing, the point is important. These two words reflect a new modern state of mind, a condition of humanity that, as it moved from a shared religious and communal language, shifted in orientation to a strong sense of individualism. While this brought us a strengthening of democracy, a greater emphasis on personal liberties and freedoms, and enhanced protection for those most vulnerable in society, it also brought us a greater emphasis on internal, individual mental states. Smith claims that both words belong to "that curious class of verbs and adjectives which describe not so much the objective qualities and activities of things as the effects they produce on us."[18] *Boring* and *interesting* as words and the expression of a new conception of engagement with the universe are roughly commensurate with the Age of the Enlightenment and with the writing of Rabbi Nachman's tale.

Language has the capacity to express a modality of existence. With the advent of a language for a specific emotion, a greater linguistic range presents itself for human expression, self-identification, and the labeling of ourselves and others. Language has an enormous power to create, generate, and stimulate behaviors and identity. Surely not everyone who uses the term *depressed* today is using it within its clinical boundaries; it is also an overdramatized way to express raging emotions without caring about medical conditions. Language can also mask or betray meaning, just as it names and affirms.

This does not mean that events, actions, and people were only interesting or boring after the advent of the words. What it does mean is that the words encapsulated feelings that were becoming more prevalent and needed a way to be articulated in the shared language of human expression. Words are the very building blocks of existence. Their importance should not be underestimated. Adam's first task in the Garden of Eden was to name the animals that were brought to him for companionship. The act of naming potentially offers greater understanding of that which is named. It is a surface portal into knowledge. Just think of how difficult medical or emotional states are when a disease goes unnamed. It seems as if without a name, these conditions cannot exist. Naming is also the way that human beings organize and thereby control (or have the illusion of control over) their worlds. Healy observes, in discussing the emergence of *boredom* as a word:

> The new term was evidently needed to give focused expression to a malaise that had increased in such degree, incidence, and reflective awareness, that it now called for a new, exact, vernacular form to replace or to substitute for the alien and only narrowly available *ennui*, and the always somewhat literary "spleen," both of which were within a relatively short time displaced by the newcomer.[19]

With the emergence of these two words, there is an affirmation of a new condition or expectation in human experience. People could become bored when there was a word to express boredom. People gradually expected their lives, social connections, and work to be interesting, since they now had a way of articulating the idea that to be interesting was a fair demand on human activity. These words did more than express individual human desires; they came to shape a host of cultural norms about modernity.

Stepping back and evaluating the impact of this linguistic revolution, it is fair to ask whether it worked. Did creating the language for boredom and interest indeed make life more boring or more interesting?

Fear and Boredom

Once given the language of boredom, we have the challenge of using it correctly. Just as the word *depression* has been thrown into common parlance and its meaning has been lightened in certain contexts, so it is with *boredom*. When we offer a crisp personal definition of religious boredom, our diagnosis leads us with greater speed to healing. Or it can lead us to a more pervasive understanding of crisis. Boredom will not be solved by finding something to do.

The fight against boredom is constant, as is well summarized in the following statement from Rabbi Israel Salanter (1810–83), one of the outstanding scholars of the Musar movement mentioned earlier: "Man may be compared to a bird. It is within the power of the bird to ascend ever higher on condition that it continues to flap its wings without cessation. Should it stop flapping for a moment, it would fall into the abyss. So it is with man."[20]

Maybe we want to be bored because it excuses us from the responsibility of generating wonder and activity, stirring curiosity, and developing within, of flapping our wings. Development involves change, and all change involves resistance. It is not hard to believe that boredom and its concomitant state of unhappiness are not actually closet desideratum that we pretend to fight. Perhaps we actually find boredom a perfectly acceptable state of existence. Philosopher Alain de Botton argues:

> There are few things humans are more dedicated to than unhappiness. Had we been placed on earth by a malign creator for the exclusive purpose of suffering, we would have good reason to congratulate ourselves on our enthusiastic response to the task. Reasons to be inconsolable abound: the frailty of our bodies, the fickleness of love, the insincerities of social life, the compromises of friendship, the deadening effects of habit. In the face of such persistent ills, we might naturally expect that no event would be awaited with greater anticipation than the moment of our extinction.[21]

Were we to actually internalize the fact that we only have this life in which to engage the world, we might fight the "deadening effects of habit" and dare to tease the boredom out of each day with a challenge to the senses and the intellect. For, to quote yet again from that masterwork *Pirkei Avot* (Ethics of the Fathers) 1:14, the ultimate statement about time's battle with boredom is actually a question: "If not now, when?"

What are we waiting for? We have analyzed the deadening impact of boredom on the Jewish soul. We have picked apart its corrosive rusting of verve in the synagogue, the boardroom, the classroom. It follows us like a lethal shadow into our offices and slips into our bedrooms and even visits us on vacation. We have come to accept it as a fact of life, and we believe that when children experience it, all the better, since it will prepare them for an adult life of tedium. We must all carry its weight like an unwanted heavy sack at all stages of human development. We have come to realize that perhaps it is we who invited this unwelcome guest into our lives. Our lethargy and lack of receptivity. Our unresponsiveness and our lack of curiosity. Our cynicism and indifference helped boredom grow like a bacteria that only in its epidemic proportions do we begin to realize how it impoverishes our lives.

But we will our boredom into existence because we may be afraid of a life that feels riskier, more thrilling, more filled with wonder. Rabbi Nachman, the same rabbi whose "simple" story we studied earlier, provides us with this reflection: "Man is afraid of things that cannot harm him and he knows it; but in truth the one thing man is afraid of is within himself, and the one thing he craves is within himself."[22]

Risk, Fate, and Boredom

Randomness is the terror that lies within us that may propel us to choose boredom. On the face of it, we complain about boredom as a malaise of habituation. We may be tired of the same food, the same school, the same job, or the same spouse. In Jewish terms, we are tired of the same community, the same group of worshippers, the same old Jewish institutions, and the same Jewish ritual objects. But in reality, what really scares us and forces us to perpetuate sameness is the fear of drastic change, the fear that one day we will wake up to a life beyond recognition. Ask any parent who has lost a child, a man who endured a divorce he never wanted who wakes up to find an empty space beside him in the morning, a woman who gives birth in her midforties after years of fertility treatments. Life changes in an instant.

Few capture this terror better than the novelist Joan Didion in her reckoning of a night in her life that changed everything for her. She and her husband had just returned home. She was in the kitchen preparing dinner. Her husband was speaking to her and then suddenly he was not. He went into cardiac arrest and died within minutes. Didion's observation hurts as it heals: "Life changes fast. Life changes in the instant. You sit down to dinner and life as you know it ends."[23] Against this emotional cataclysm, we would take boredom any day. We welcome boredom, invite it into our lives willingly.

We do hear people say, "I wish my life were more boring," but we never believe them, in part because the people who say things like this seem to have fantastically interesting lives. They only say that they want a slower, less interesting pace to make the rest of us feel better. But sometimes people say this without saying it. They feel great despair at life conditions they never would have expected, and their faces cry out with a request for emotional simplicity.

The gift of religion is not that it makes such dramatic events go away but that it eases the harsh edges of them by ritualizing life-cycle moments and bringing us into the embrace of community. We cannot escape divine fate; we can only surround ourselves with sentiments, people, and traditions that will slow it all down, force us to confront and digest change, and offer us relief from isolation when we do. That these very life supports bore us at times is, well, a relatively minor sacrifice. Judaism, at its very best, offers us mechanisms to jog curiosity, stimulate study, experience gratitude for the smallest of gifts, consider history and relive it, ritualize important moments and do that within community. It tries to remove the patina of boredom by offering us a legal system, a rich culture and history, and a social network should we choose to accept and live by it. Judaism gives us the armor and the company to face our greatest primal fears and losses.

The Authentic Jewish Self

Diane Ackerman contends that the genuine self is the person we find when life's circumstances change radically: "There is a point beyond which the senses cannot lead us. Ecstasy means being flung out of your usual self, but that is still to feel a commotion inside.... If we are in a rut, it is a palatial and exquisite rut."[24]

We are a holder of experiences, an ark and a sanctuary, that is Ackerman's "exquisite rut." In Rabbi Soloveitchik's words:

> The sanctuary of the human person is his life, not his logical life. The Ark is with us in each person's emotional life, concealed behind the curtain. This aspect of the human being is protected from the eye of the cynic, the glance of the skeptic, the ridicule of the so-called practical and realistic man.[25]

The human ark is a fragile entity that needs constant protection from the cynic and the critic. It also requires nurturing and exposure to forces that will strengthen it and let it grow. If we do not know what we are missing in the realm of wonder, then we must make that leap of faith, to believe that our boredom is not the whole story, that there are people who experience the marvel and astonishment of Judaism, and that they may have the willingness to teach us or let us observe them. Fromm comments:

> One aspect of religious experience is the wondering, the marveling, the becoming aware of life and one's own existence, and of the puzzling problem of one's relatedness to the world.... One who has never been bewildered, who has never looked upon life and his own existence as phenomena which require answers and yet, paradoxically, for which the only answers are new questions, can hardly understand what religious experience is.[26]

We are not responsible for fixing every Jewish problem. At the very least, we must recognize the boredom within our lives and realize that it is a problem that requires our concern. We must believe that we can make a difference.

Robert Nozick, an American philosopher and professor at Harvard University, reflected on this notion in his book *The Examined Life*. For him, "being more real" is accepting that our lives continue through experimentation and modification. We recognize that there are places and people who make us feel more real, more authentic, than others. We feel real when we are alert and focused or "dwelling in unaccustomed emotions" or in contact with parts of ourselves not frequently "visited." In other words, paradoxically, we find ourselves most authentic precisely when we encounter the unfamiliar in ourselves. It is not familiarity with the self that breeds authenticity, and it is certainly not glib happiness. "Our reality consists partly in the values we pursue and live by, the vividness, intensity and integration with which we embody them."[27] We all want to live lives in color. We can only do that when we come to terms with our own responsibility for making life colorful. French mathematician Blaise Pascal believed that "the sole cause of man's unhappiness is that he does not know how to stay quietly in his room."[28] Rabbi Adin Steinsaltz, a noted Israeli scholar, author, philosopher, and translator of the Talmud, believes that the kind of vivid intensity we crave will only be ours when we recognize our essential aloneness in the world:

> The search for the self, in other words, the search for the essence, the inwardness, and the way of the soul, stems from the recognition that one is alone in the world. When man stands suddenly alone in the world, when everything seems to be addressed only to him, then there is no aspect of reality that does not challenge him.... It would appear that the real agony begins when one's horizons in this world expand.... With external reality pressing heavily on man, the physical, the philosophical, the psychological questions only intensify the urgency of the basic question of self. And yet very often it seems that the basic point, the self, is untouched—even though the more a person grows, the more the problem of the self should also grow....

The seeker is caught in a paradox. He is dismayed to learn that the resolution of the search for the self is not to be found by going into the self, that the center of the soul is to be found not in the soul but outside of it, that the center of gravity of existence is outside of existence.[29]

There is an error that we make, believing that the self can only be understood within, that I will find myself by examining myself. We find ourselves when we engage in something much larger than self. According to Nozick:

> We are not merely empty buckets to be stuffed with happiness or pleasure; the self's nature and character matter, too, even matter more. It is easy to fall into an "end-state" conception of the self, demarcating some particular condition for it to reach and maintain. As important as the self's constituents and structure, however, are the ways it transforms itself.... The self does not simply undergo these processes, it shapes and chooses them, it initiates and runs them. Part of the self's value dwells in its ability to transform *itself* and so be self-creating.[30]

We have the tremendous possibility of personal transformation, becoming the self we really want to be or *returning* to a sense of personal authenticity. Holiness is a human construct; we make it. We define its boundaries. We determine its meaning. And, if we are lucky, we live within a spiritual tradition that guides us to finding greater meaning in everyday living by enhancing the mystery of it all, as Diane Ackerman concludes:

> It began in mystery, and it will end in mystery. However many of life's large, captivating principles and small, captivating details we may explore, unpuzzle, and learn by heart, there will be vast unknown realms to lure us.... When there is no emotional risk, the emotional terrain is flat and unyielding and, despite all its dimensions, valleys, pinnacles and detours, life

will seem to have none of its magnificent geography, only a length. It began in mystery, and it will end in mystery, but what a savage and beautiful country lies in between.[31]

It is time to take some spiritual risks. It is time to invite childhood curiosity back into our lives. Judaism can be the savage and beautiful country of mystery. It's our choice.

10 An End to Boredom– Some Practical Advice

> I've got a great ambition to die of exhaustion
> rather than boredom.
>
> *Thomas Carlyle*

Can there ever be an end to boredom, or have we welcomed a term into our cultural lexicon that will always be there, staring at us like a clock does at an interminably long meeting? The previous nine chapters have been descriptive. We have explored the etiology of boredom and its linguistic, even "medical" origins. We have tried to define boredom and explore its nature through the study of philosophy and theology, Jewish prayer, community, and education. We examined the need for wonder and the craving for authenticity. Our conversations, however, have not been prescriptive.

There will never be an end to boredom, but with planning and insight, we may get closer to managing it, leveraging it, and allowing it to teach us something about ourselves. There are practical recommendations that can both spare us from the gigantic gulf of restlessness and ennui and also generate greater creativity and productivity. Our most pedestrian moments can have greater heft, depth, and meaning. Here are ten *practical* ways to minimize or eliminate boredom, followed by three frameworks for changing our attitude to boredom.

Not Ten Commandments, Just Ten Suggestions

Drop the Language of Boredom

Language both describes reality and creates it. We have a language of boredom, and unless we excise it, we are in danger of letting it color experience. We are the generation that invented the expression "Been there, done that," one of the most pernicious summations of human experience. It implies that there is nothing to be gained by a repeat performance. It means that one-time experiences, events, and feelings are sufficient. There are no books worth reading again, movies worth a second view, and places that we might want to revisit. There are no spiritual experiences worth deepening. It's time to let go of the words we use to describe boredom, recognizing that they limit us. Next time you find yourself about to say the *b* word, as in "I'm bored," or the *b* expression, as in "Been there, done that," catch yourself. Catch your kids saying it. Find another way to say it, or better yet, don't find another way to say it. Drop it.

Ten Times Two

The Harvard School of Education's "Project Zero" is geared to help teachers explore the world of multiple intelligences. One of the exercises promoted in this project is "ten times two." Look at something once and identify ten things you notice. You may be standing in front of a painting, sitting before a book, or analyzing a conversation with a friend. Just when it seems impossible to get to ten, try to locate ten more things. You'll find that this exercise feels torturous until the moment it feels wonderful. Wonder requires digging deeper, seeing more, and expanding the way that we think. Boredom is limiting. Ten times two is a simple exercise that opens up the way that we experience the world.

Do Something That Scares You

Eleanor Roosevelt once famously said, "Do something every day that scares you." While I'm not suggesting you go skydiving tomorrow (although not a bad idea), I am recommending that you embrace experiences that you've never had, especially those that involve some element of risk, physical or emotional. Within the realm of the spiritual, there is always a range of behaviors and emotions that we have yet to experience. Close your eyes when you pray. Meditate. Fast. Study the Talmud with a great teacher. Dance quickly in the middle circle of a Jewish wedding. The adrenaline rush will convince you that life is not boring. We are.

The Triumph of Social Justice

There is a lot in the world to protest: world poverty, genocide in Africa, homelessness in our own cities. There is hardly an experience less boring and more purposeful than fighting on behalf of someone else. Judaism has a strong tradition of calling attention to the plight of others because "we were strangers" (Exodus 22:20). We know alienation firsthand, and we are obligated not to let injustice corrupt our beautiful world. So "justice, justice you shall pursue" (Deuteronomy 16:20) and you won't complain a moment about having nothing to do.

Smile When You Pray

Simple facial gestures and expressions can alter the way that we experience life. Don't wait until there is something to smile about. Smile and you may just create something to smile about. Write down an original prayer of thanksgiving and smile when you read it. Allow the feeling of being blessed to permeate your being. Blessed people don't feel bored. They feel that they can smile because they believe that someone is smiling down on them. In response, they pray. Prayer does not have to be something that someone else wrote in a different language whose words we cannot understand. It can be the sincere outpouring of a heart on fire. Your heart.

Create More Space for Yourself

Spiritual boredom may really be a cry for time and space for ourselves. Family and community can have a hijacking quality. Other people seem to want something from us all of the time, diminishing time for reflection and self-direction. The boredom of doing the same thing for the same people again and again can be reduced by scheduling time for yourself every day to do something spiritually satisfying, something that generates purpose. I know women who would never miss their weekly pedicure, men who would never miss a day on the treadmill. Staving off spiritual boredom requires daily discipline. Be spiritually selfish. Just a little.

Minimize Distractions

In this age of electronic devices, people can find us all the time, and we can be "connected" all the time. But to what are we connected? The reactive society that e-mails and cell phones have created has left us less time to be proactive. That's true in our spiritual lives as well. The word *hineni* in the Hebrew Bible is the one-word expression of readiness for a spiritual calling. Instead of translating it as "I am here," think of it as "I am fully present." Ask yourself when you're multitasking whether you are fully present in your life. It's easy to feel bored when you've never been fully present in the first place.

Open a Jewish Book and Find Yourself a Teacher

Within Jewish tradition, there is perhaps no experience lauded as more purposeful than Jewish study. We don't let our minds atrophy or believe that Jewish learning is something for children only. Quite the contrary. Jewish study has always been considered a purview of the adult mind. Today, with so many classes available, it's a wonder that more people do not avail themselves of the treasure of Jewish learning. It creates a community of people around ideas; it helps us understand why faith matters and how to navigate the complex milestones and losses of adult life. It freights rituals we already observe with meaning.

Set the Table

There can be few rituals more spiritually enhancing than Shabbat dinner. The time with family and friends, the conversations, the good food and smells, the pause, and the spiritual intimacy of a Shabbat meal are hard to replicate or even describe. You have to participate in one to understand its benefits. Once a week, in a universe of chaos and demands on our time, we stand apart from the clock and enter an island of serenity. The forced stop begins to answer the meaning deficit we experience in our spiritual lives. Nothing boring about that. Shabbat is a time when the clothes, food, and talk should be elevated and different. If you've been having Shabbat meals for years, try something new at the table. Invite people who are very different from those in your social circle. Try new recipes. Put different typewritten questions under everyone's plate, and ask people to answer their questions between courses. Just as we make Shabbat different from other days of the week, we should also try to make Shabbat dinners distinct and memorable.

Listen with Your Eyes

There is a biblical expression that appears multiple times to describe the ultimate encounter with the other: *panim el panim*, "face to face." God speaks to Moses face to face. When we really confront someone this way, we open a profound capacity for relatedness and holiness. In his book *Seek My Face: A Jewish Mystical Theology* (Jewish Lights), Arthur Green, professor and dean of the Rabbinical School at Boston's Hebrew College, tells of a Hasidic master, Rabbi Nachman Kossover, who used to see the sacred letters of God's name on the faces of everyone he spoke with, encountering each person as if he or she were created in God's image.[1] We don't listen enough with our eyes, writing off people too quickly as boring before we get to know them, before we find the divinity in them. The more we open ourselves to others with honesty and vulnerability and the more we make room for them, the more we will bring an added sense of purpose to each day. Rabbi Nachman's technique of creating a divine lens with which to see others and God can help us manage ourselves and our relationships better, especially when we think someone else is boring. We may just not be listening with our eyes.

Those are ten recommendations. They hardly exhaust a full list of possibilities. I invite you to make your own. No one can control your own spiritual boredom the way you can. In addition to practical recommendations, we also need to look at some overall attitudes that help shape meaning and minimize boredom: sanctifying time, teaching ourselves stillness, and using boredom as a lever to creativity, what we'll call generative boredom.

Sanctifying Time

We know cognitively that time always passes at the same rate; nevertheless, there seems to be an immense difference between how quickly time goes by when we are enjoying ourselves and how slowly it goes by when we are not. We can all remember college professors who seemed to stop the clock; we intuitively doodled or wrote notes to a neighbor to salvage the time. We weren't really redeeming wasted moments with our scribbles; we were just passing time.

There are actually important neurological changes taking place during moments of boredom that may offer us an insight into boredom's relief. At times when we find ourselves nodding off, "the brain has concluded there is nothing new or useful it can learn from an environment, a person, an event, a paragraph."[2] And yet, according to Benedict Carey, in our mind's eye

> it is far from a neural shrug. Using brain-imaging technology, neurologists have found that the brain is highly active when disengaged, consuming about five percent less energy in its resting "default state" than when involved in routine tasks … the slight reduction can make a big difference in terms of time perception. The seconds usually seem to pass more slowly when the brain is idling than when it is absorbed. And those stretched seconds are not the live-in-the-moment, meditative variety, either. They are frustrated, restless moments.[3]

Scientific studies are, in essence, suggesting that there really is a difference between an idling mind and an absorbed mind in terms of the passage of time. Boredom *must* be relieved and begs for a constructive response. We can actually make time pass more quickly by finding a way to engage ourselves and make the most of a tedious moment.

Judaism is a faith structure that advises sanctifying time, not merely passing it. Sanctifying time means that we create opportunities for a full range of emotions. In art, a painting of full values expresses a color from its lightest to its darkest shade. A green palette that goes from mint to olive and every shade in between makes the painting a reflection of real life: complex, rich, interesting, and multidimensional. We find this richness, this fullness, everywhere we turn in Judaism. The Jewish calendar year and milestone rituals invite us into "spectrum" experiences, from personal and national mourning to the celebration of ancient harvests and adolescent growth spurts. Across the life span and across the heart-strings, Judaism asks us to stop and take note, to reflect in community and in private prayer, and, most importantly, to act. In Judaism, we don't merely scribble through time. We orchestrate time with intentionality.

Rabbi Eliezer prescribed in *Pirkei Avot* (Ethics of the Fathers) 2:6 that we repent the day before we die. The obvious question is how do we know when we are at death's door. We don't. Rabbi Eliezer gives us a paradigm shift to reshape everyday living. If this were your last day, would you scribble through it? If this were your last conversation with a child, a friend, a spouse, would you have used those words, that tone of voice? Because, at the end of day, how do you know that it is not your last day?

And Rabbi Eliezer informs us of another truth about Judaism. We are given the potential to repent every day. Choice and change are powers handed to us from the very first chapters of Genesis and from the first day of every Jewish year. Many people believe that Rosh Hashanah is the anniversary of the birth of the world. It isn't. In Jewish liturgy it is described as the actual day of creation itself. There is a majestic sense that the world is allowed to renew itself annually, both repeating a well-established pattern and also energizing all of creation with another chance, a new birth.

Teaching Ourselves to Be Still

Along with the capacity to sanctify time and help it move more quickly, we also need the ability to stay still to end boredom. We have all had times in our personal and professional lives where we pushed ourselves literally or figuratively to keep moving, do more, distract ourselves, and stay awake. At some point, we stop and then suddenly feel terribly tired. While in motion, we felt ourselves almost invincible. We didn't need sleep. We didn't need to eat. We seemed to have an endless supply of energy. Then a few minutes of downtime was all it took to realize how exhausted we really were.

Imagine that this is true not only when we are pushing ourselves intentionally in certain specific ways but in the general push of daily life.

We may break so infrequently to reflect that when we do, we actually find ourselves falling asleep. A friend dragged her husband to a meditation class. The teacher dimmed the lights to near blackness and lit a small candle, asking everyone to lie quietly on a mat. My friend was awfully embarrassed when she suddenly heard the loud snoring of her husband. He claims that he was just in close contact with his deepest inner needs.

If we go from constant movement to deep sleeping, we miss the quiet moments altogether. We call them boredom, but they're actually just stations that stop us along the way and help us check in, because we are not made to work or think or move all the time. We gain some perspective on boredom as a pause from the English social reformer Bertrand Russell. He held many unconventional views and took on any number of controversial and unusual topics before they were faddish, like happiness.

Today, hardly a month goes by without a new treatise on happiness. Russell understood almost a hundred years ago the corrupting dangers of a society enmeshed in an energetic search for perpetual satisfaction and immediate gratification, and also understood the impact that this need has on boredom. Originally published in 1930, Russell's book *The Conquest of Happiness* sounds almost militaristic. Russell attacks boredom and believes that it is one of the "great motive powers," perhaps today more than ever.[4] Animals, he claims, may pace up and down, but they do not experience anything analogous to boredom.

> One of the essentials of boredom consists in the contrast between present circumstances which force themselves irresistibly upon the imagination. It is also one of the essentials of boredom that one's faculties must not be fully occupied. Running away from enemies who are trying to take one's life is, I imagine, unpleasant, but certainly not boring. A man would not feel bored while he was being executed.[5]

Russell offers us the challenge of being intensely engaged, the way we might at the brink of death, a feeling that would paradoxically make us feel powerfully alive.

A friend was sharing his fear about a journey to visit a seemingly dangerous neighborhood in the Middle East; everyone he saw looked suspicious. The political and military surroundings were deeply frightening. He felt intimately aware of every move he made and even the subtle movements of all those around him. His fear alerted and informed the movements of every part of his body. His eyes and ears were totally radar focused on his environment in ways that he had not previously experienced. Suddenly, trailed by the fear of death, he realized that he had never felt himself to be more alive.

Russell contends that the need to avoid boredom is primal. "The desire for excitement is very deep-seated in human beings, especially in males."[6] Should we think we live in boring times, Russell offers a brief history of boredom to comfort us. Early human life was filled with conquest and savagery. Then the agrarian lifestyle suppressed excitement. Russell asks us to imagine midwinter in a medieval village. The monotony, the lack of light, the impassable road conditions all led to isolation and restlessness. But today, we are "less bored than our ancestors were, but we are more afraid of boredom."[7]

Our need to avoid boredom increases with our rise in the social scale because more opportunities for entertainment and education present themselves with an increase in wealth. Russell divides boredom into two categories: fructifying and stultifying. Fructifying boredom is caused by the absence of drugs. Stultifying boredom is caused by the lack of vital activity. In combination, the result is deadly. Many narcotics create moments of effortless pleasure that require ever-increasing intensity to achieve the same level of satisfaction. Remove the stimulus, and boredom magically appears again. Consequently, when excitement is produced by any physical stimulus, the stakes must be raised simply to stay at the same level of entertainment. This may manifest itself as an increase in sexual stimulation, in the amount of alcohol in a drinking binge, or in the level of violence in video games or movies. Once upon a time, people in films died by being shot. Today, they are thrown from planes, land on the antennae of skyscrapers, get thrown into a human food processor and ground into hamburgers. It takes a lot to impress us.

The need for constant and ever-elevating excitement is pernicious and ultimately destructive. According to Russell:

> A life too full of excitement is an exhausting life, in which continually stronger stimuli are needed to give the thrill that has come to be thought of as an essential part of pleasure.... There is an element of boredom which is inseparable from the avoidance of too much excitement, and too much excitement not only undermines the health, but dulls the palate for every kind of pleasure, substituting titillations for profound organic satisfactions, cleverness for wisdom, and jagged surprises for excitement.[8]

This fear of boredom has presented many challenges to the moral life, although ultimately Russell claims, "Perhaps some element of boredom is a necessary ingredient in life."[9] We need to teach ourselves to sit still, to understand the difference between boredom and calm. Our repose is valuable in and of itself, and it also helps as a way station and preparation for times of greater excitement.

Nowhere is this perhaps more true than in an electrifying biblical text (1 Kings 18–19). Elijah, a prophet renowned for zealotry and intensity, challenges Ahab, the reigning king, to a spiritual duel. Ahab gathers all his pagan prophets, four hundred and fifty strong, to Mount Carmel to confront Elijah's God with Baal and to see who is to be victorious. Elijah hates any middle-of-the-road behavior and reproaches his own people to be consistent: "How long will you straddle two fences? If the Lord is God, follow Him. If Baal is god, follow him" (1 Kings 18:21). To this, the people say nothing. Elijah tells the prophets of Baal to shout louder when their god is not attentive and works the crowd into an absolute frenzy. Elijah wins the competition and has the prophets killed, but it is a pyrrhic victory. Jezebel, Ahab's wife, is determined to have Elijah murdered as a result. Elijah flees the area and runs in the direction of the wilderness. He comes to a tree, halts there, and asks God to take his life instead.

Everything about the story is high drama. There is noise and tension, incredible pressure, and existential questioning. Elijah finally falls into a deep sleep. He wakes up to find a meal left for him by an angel and then, like Moses at Sinai, refuses food for forty days and nights. He goes into a cave. Slowly, he seems to be removing himself from this world. It is at this point that God calls him to a mountain for an act of revelation. The appearance matches none of the intensity of the last chapters. It seems almost anticlimactic. But it is in this pause that Elijah finally finds future direction, and it is in this moment of recovery and solitude that Elijah experiences God personally:

> There was a great and mighty wind, splitting mountains and shattering rocks by the power of the Lord; but the Lord was not in the wind. After the wind—an earthquake; but the Lord was not in the earthquake. After the earthquake—fire; but the Lord was not in the fire. And after the fire—a lone, thin voice.
> (1 Kings 19:11–12)

That lone, thin voice dictates the directive that Elijah appoint his successor. It is this text that forms a core sentiment of one of our most famous pieces of High Holy Day worship, *Unetaneh Tokef*. Without its biblical context, it is no longer understood as central to Elijah's search for leadership; it is a statement about the very power of prayer. Prayer is ultimately not about the spiritual crescendos and the loud noise of imposed piety. It is about humility and vulnerability. It is about the quiet between the drama. In the words of Chaplain Susan Cosio, "Prayer, I have discovered, is less about what I say and more about what I hear."[10] What everyone else regards as insignificant and even boring is, in fact, often the transition between dramas that makes excitement possible.

Generative Boredom

In *Against Happiness*, professor and author Eric Wilson, like Russell but almost eighty years later, bemoans the contemporary fascination and preoccupation with happiness. He believes that melancholy is life's mentor, and without it, dimensions of happiness are also sacrificed. He calls sadness "generative melancholia."

It is our own nervous fear, our melancholia, that leads to our awareness of the world's innate duplicity, its "both/and." Only by being unwilling to rest on one side of the world or the other do we come to sense the hidden marriage between both sides. Sadly inhabiting this rich limbo, we put ourselves in a position to grasp the profound meaning of life's deepest events. These vexed events reveal to us what is already true of everything; all creatures are meldings of grandeur and gloom.[11]

This dichotomous picture creates a world of emotional opposites. Grandeur and gloom present a precarious and extreme scale with which to measure a life. And while we might find ourselves in this dialectic adding meaning to these polar expressions of human emotion, they fail to represent the actual day-to-day experiences of life.

More accurate would be to ask us to think of all of the moments in between the poles, the lone, thin voice of God from Mount Carmel. Times that seem unemotional and uninformative can actually become daily doses of generative boredom. Why wait for melancholia to generate thoughtfulness and insight? Perhaps the boredom of it all can prove more instructive and realistic. Our challenge is to make the prosaic, if not sacred, then at least a lever to creativity.

Joseph Brodsky takes this notion of generative boredom one step further. In the two hundred and nineteenth commencement address at Dartmouth College, this poet and winner of the Nobel Prize for Literature told his young and ambitious audience that they have a lifetime of boredom to look forward to when they leave the college grounds. He called boredom "a substantial part of what lies ahead."[12] This is so strikingly different from the message that most college graduates are given. The world is your oyster. *Carpe diem.* With each throw of a graduation cap, this new adult workforce is to embrace life. Take risks. Live every moment. What kind of commencement address tells students that what lies ahead is largely vast spaces of empty time? Why bother leaving the university quadrangle for that?

Brodsky gets worse before he gets better. "When hit by boredom, go for it. Let yourself be crushed by it." Brodsky, naturally, qualifies his message. "For boredom speaks the language of time, and it is to teach you the most valuable lesson of your life: the lesson of utter insignificance."[13] If college graduates did not want to hear that boredom awaits them in the adult world post-university, surely they do not want to learn that they matter not at all. But Brodsky spoke as a true poet. He called insignificance a privilege because it is this sentiment that "grows sensitivity to the outer world, a sense of mortality, and ultimately, passion."[14]

When boredom overtakes you and you confront the futility of human life, you suddenly embrace that which is most precious, and this nearness to death teaches you how to be alive. Without a sense of mortality, there would be no poetry. There would be no sense of the exquisite detail and fragility of it all. To get the full flavor of this existential angst from a Jewish perspective, we turn to the words of prayer during our holiest of seasons. In the *Musaf*, or additional service for Rosh Hashanah and Yom Kippur, we are immersed in our mortality. We are, in Brodsky's words, crushed by it. In the words of Fromm:

> Man, his beginning is from dust and ends in dust; risking his life, he gets his bread, he is like pottery that is breakable, like grass that withers, like the flower that fades, like the shadow that passes, like the cloud that vanishes, like the wind that blows, like the dust that flies, and like a fleeting dream.[15]

We are trapped in the mundane tasks of self-preservation, knowing all along that we will return to the very earth that we rely on for our sustenance. Everything about us and around us is in a stage of decay and disappearance. And as we stand in synagogue and sing these words in the company of a congregation, we tremble with the privilege of insignificance. Nothing could be more apparent at these moments of prayer than our nothingness. And then we come to the final words of the passage: "But you are the King, the Almighty, the everlasting God." We contrast our impermanence with God's sustaining presence. We compare what we are to what God is not. And the congregation that says the earlier words with meekness and temerity suddenly bursts forth with this statement of surety. Brodsky nailed the sentiment. The person in this prayer is not discovering the cure for cancer. He is not traveling to Mars. She is not even writing a poem. The person in this prayer is just trying to get through the day, fading like a flower, passing like a shadow, fleeting as a dream.

Generative boredom is the kind of boredom that we grow until it becomes our most stalwart and persistent teacher. Rather than dismiss it as an insignificant emotion, we need to grab on to it and feel it fully so that we can get to the other side of it. As it takes over our minds and looms over our behaviors and actions, it becomes our touchstone with what is most real, what is most significant.

How do we tend to the religious mind that is bored and distracted? William James described the state of religious boredom as the "sick soul." The sick soul is not necessarily a problem as much as a regular but uninvited guest that we must learn how to accommodate. We know that the visitor will be arriving, thus we can prepare accordingly. To take this conversation one step further, there are religious thinkers who believe that boredom is an "essential precondition for the imagination's exercise."[16] We need to be bored. When we get bored and take responsibility for our boredom, we arrive at a new level of interest, introspection, or action that has been stirred by the very creativity used to keep boredom away. The relationship between boredom and creativity is far from accidental. Creative minds are often stimulated by boredom, regarding it as a brain rest until the next great idea looms on the horizon of the otherwise unoccupied mind.

John Gardner, former Secretary of Health, Education, and Welfare and the author of *Self-Renewal* among many other works, observed that more people are bored in their everyday lives than are willing to admit:

> Boredom is the secret ailment of modern life. A successful executive said to me the other day, "How can I be so bored when I'm so busy?" And I said, "Let me count the ways." Logan Pearsall Smith said that boredom can rise to the level of a mystical experience, and if that's true I know some very busy adults who are among the great mystics of all time.[17]

Essential Nothingness

Much like ancient Chinese mental puzzles, Kabbalah engages us precisely by seeming to contradict itself or confuse us. If we can make our way through the confusion, we may just find enlightenment. Nothing is really something.

> The depth of primordial being is called Boundless. Because of its concealment from all creatures above and below, it is also called Nothingness. If one asks, "What is it?" the answer is "Nothing," meaning: No one can understand anything about it. It is negated of every conception. No one can know anything about it—except the belief that it exists. Its existence cannot be grasped by anyone other than it. Therefore its name is "I am becoming."[18]

What are we to make of what sounds like mystical chatter? In Kabbalah, absence is presence. The fact that something is invisible and incomprehensible does not make it nonexistent as a substance to be reckoned with, prodded, or studied. A white wall is not blank; it is white. A blank notebook is not nothing; it is something. This wordplay asks for the recognition of active emptiness so that we can we begin the process of filling, much as an empty glass asks, by virtue of its emptiness, to be filled and an empty bench asks for company. In other words, the blankness that we feel may actually be more like an empty chalkboard waiting for notation or a white canvas that invites paint. It is nothingness on the way to becoming somethingness. Boredom can be the mental beginnings of something very beautiful.

Boredom as Teacher

We began with Ecclesiastes, and with Ecclesiastes we shall end. As early as chapter 1 of this meditation on futility, we read that even that which we think is new and innovative is only really a repetition of what was done earlier:

> Sometimes there is a phenomenon of which they say, "Look, this one is new!"—it occurred long ago, in ages that went by before us. The earlier ones are not remembered; so, too, those that will occur later will no more be remembered than those that will occur at the very end. (Ecclesiastes 1:10–11)

What can we create that is new? It has all been done before. We are subjected to boredom at every turn because of the impossibility of newness. This is the voice of despair.

We all have moments when we believe that there is no new contribution to be made, no change that is possible, nothing that has not yet been discovered. And yet, everyday people do discover that which is new. We have insights into human nature; we learn that people are not always who we thought they were. We discover new and more efficient ways of doing things. We invent and build upon that which came before us.

In the medieval period, a number of Jewish Rabbinic experts adapted an expression found in Christian scholasticism to justify disagreeing with earlier scholars. Rabbinic Judaism is predicated on a belief that scholarship that is closest in time to the revelation at Sinai is also the most authoritative. How, then, could anyone write a new book of Jewish law? Such thinking stops the flow of intellectual progress. Jewish law, however, is termed *halakha*, from the Hebrew root word "to go forth," to progress, to advance. For later scholars, this tension was captured and resolved by acknowledging the greatness of the experts before them while justifying, ever so slightly, their ability to add to this complex tradition of scholarship: "They were giants. We are dwarfs. But dwarfs on the shoulders of giants can see farther than giants." Our capacity for newness is not in being wholly original but in leveraging the work of the past to see beyond it, even just a little bit. Through this formula we recast our ability to create, invent, and discover that which is new.

We are propelled forward, to drill through boredom rather than sidestep it, by this capacity for incremental newness that can be learned only when we make boredom our teacher. We need to sit with boredom long enough to get bored of boredom. And then, when we have become totally consumed by that which is uninteresting and disengaging, we may find ourselves on the magical brink of great discovery and change. This sense that the future will somehow be like and unlike the past is a mystery, captured again, in the words of Ecclesiastes: "A man cannot know what will happen: who can know what the future holds?" (Ecclesiastes 10:14).

Despite the futility that is stamped and decried all over Ecclesiastes, King Solomon, its attributed author, still acknowledged the space for humans to overcome tedium, to learn from boredom. He believed in the power of *mitzvah*, of commandedness, to elevate and offer purpose to humanity. Solomon, who had excessive wisdom, women, and wealth and could find little use for any of them by the end of his life, still had the gumption to declare, "Whatever is in your power to do, do with all your might" (Ecclesiastes 9:10).

Our challenge today is to make boredom a true emotion, a Solomonic emotion, a Brodsky emotion, and not a merely a trivial lack of entertainment, a spiritual pocket in which to put idle hands. Boredom must be deeply experienced as a significant and conscious awareness that inspires insignificance to force spiritual creativity. Only through authentic boredom can we learn to live in the spaces between nothing and something. And in between those spaces lies our transcendence.

NOTES

I. Solomon's Spleen: Defining Boredom

1. Although contemporary Bible scholarship questions Solomon as the author of Ecclesiastes, the Sages of the Talmud attributed this book to his authorship.
2. Gary Rosenblatt (editor of *The Jewish Week*), quoted in Josh Lipowsky, "UJA-NNJ Announces New Path at Meeting," *New Jersey Jewish Standard,* June 30, 2007, based on keynote speech June 20, 2007, at Temple Emmanuel, Woodcliff Lake, NJ.
3. Gary Rosenblatt, quoted in Jonathan Mark, www.lukeford.net/profiles (June 30, 2007).
4. Bruce Leckart, with L. G. Weinberger, *Up from Boredom, Down from Fear* (New York: Richard Marek, 1980), 32.
5. Ibid., 31.
6. Sean Desmond Healy, *Boredom, Self and Culture* (Cranbury, NJ: Associated University Presses, 1984), 16.
7. Dylan Thomas, in Rayner Heppenstall, *Four Absentees* (London: Barrie and Rockliff, 1960), 139.
8. Erich Fromm, *The Anatomy of Human Destructiveness* (Greenwich, CT: Fawcett, 1973), 274.
9. Sigmond Shore, "The Wake Up Tour," on JSPS.com, *The Jewish Student Press Service: New Voices: Campus Report*, June 9, 2007.
10. Matthew Green, in *Minor Poets of the Eighteenth Century*, ed. Hugh l'Anson Fausset (London: J. M. Dent and Sons, 1930), 211.
11. Healy, *Boredom, Self and Culture*, 22.
12. Martin Heidegger, "What Is Metaphysics?" in *Existence and Being*, ed. W. Brock (Chicago: Henry Regnery, 1949), 364.
13. Immanuel Kant, "Padagogik," *Kants gesammelte Schriften* (Berlin and New York, 1902), 9:471.
14. Friedrich Nietzsche, "Der Antichrist," *Kritische Studienausgabe* (Munich Berlin, New York 1988), 6:48.

15. Teresa Belton and Esther Priyadharshini, "Boredom and Schooling: A Cross-disciplinary Perspective," *Cambridge Journal of Education* 37, no. 4 (2007): 579–95.
16. Benedict Carey, "You're Checked Out, but Your Brain Is Tuned In," *New York Times*, August 5, 2008.
17. Bertrand Russell, *The Conquest of Happiness* (New York: Liveright, 1930), 56.
18. Lars Svendsen, *A Philosophy of Boredom*, trans. John Irons (London: Reaktion Books, 2005), 8.
19. Ibid., 7.
20. Arthur Schopenhauer, *Essays and Aphorisms* (New York: Penguin Classics, 2004), 53.
21. Heidegger, *What Is Metaphysics?* Espen Hammer analyzes Heidegger's approach to boredom in "Heidegger's Theory of Boredom," *Graduate Faculty Philosophy Journal* 29, no. 1 (2008): 199–227.
22. Patricia Meyer Spacks, *Boredom: The Literary History of a State of Mind* (Chicago: University of Chicago Press, 1995), 6.
23. Orrin Klapp, *Overload and Boredom: Essays on the Quality of Life in the Information Society* (New York: Greenwood, 1986), 23–24, quoted in Spacks, *Boredom*, 3.
24. Spacks, *Boredom*, 23.
25. Ibid., 272.
26. Viktor E. Frankl, *Man's Search for Meaning*, trans. Ilse Lasch (Boston: Beacon Press, 1992), 105.

2. Embracing the Lion: Acedia and Spiritual Fatigue

1. Michael Raposa, *Boredom and the Religious Imagination* (Charlottesville, VA: University Press of Virginia, 1999), 11–12.
2. *Shulhan Arukh, Orekh Haim* 1:1.
3. Israel Meir Kagen, *Mishnah Berurah, Orekh Haim* 1:1.
4. Sol Schimmel, *The Seven Deadly Sins: Jewish, Christian and Classical Reflections on Human Nature* (New York: Free Press, 1992), 202–3.
5. Moshe Hayyim Luzzatto, *The Path of the Just* (Jerusalem: Feldheim, 1966), 79.
6. I am grateful to Sol Schimmel for this source, found on p. 203 of *The Seven Deadly Sins* without attribution.
7. Susan Sontag, in Jill Krementz, *The Writer's Desk* (New York: Random House, 1996), 17.
8. Carleton Parker, *The Casual Laborer and Other Essays* (New York: Harcourt, Brace and Howe, 1920).
9. Raposa, *Boredom and the Religious Imagination*, 37–38.

3. The Hermeneutics of Boredom

1. Paul Ricoeur, *Freud and Philosophy: An Essay on Interpretation* (New Haven: Yale University Press, 1970), 33.

2. Ruel Pepa, "Nurturing the Imagination of Resistance: Some Important Views from Contemporary Philosophers" (2004 Martin Heidegger Memorial Lecture, Trinity College of Quezon City, Philippines, July 28, 2004). Pupa writes of the hermeneutics of suspicion: "It suspects the credibility of the superficial text and explores what is underneath the surface to reveal a more authentic dimension of meaning. It is only in destroying the false assumptions and the untenable platforms of awareness that new liberating paradigms of thought may arise to allow the human being a better interpretation of her/his reality. In the process, such hermeneutics of suspicion leads to a bi-focal critique—a critique that is not only trained towards the participant in a system but likewise towards the system itself."

3. Patricia Meyer Spacks, *Boredom: The Literary History of a State of Mind* (Chicago: University of Chicago Press, 1995), 6.

4. Ibid., 6.

5. Ibid., 1. Spacks continues, "The need to refute boredom's deadening power impels the writer's productivity and the reader's engagement. In the best of all possible arrangements, an author's energy and a reader's reciprocate.... The mutual dependence of writer and reader declares their human likeness in shared defiance of psychic entropy."

6. A. S. Byatt, *Possession* (New York: Modern Library, 2001), 558–59.

7. Marcel Proust, in Alain de Botton, *How Proust Can Change Your Life* (New York: Vintage International, 1997), 24–25.

8. Alain de Botton, *The Consolations of Philosophy* (New York: Vintage International, 2000), 158.

9. Svendsen, *Philosophy of Boredom*, 116–132.

10. Ibid., 119.

11. Leckart, *Up from Boredom, Down from Fear,* 38.

12. Ibid., 43.

13. Irwin Edman, "Peace," in *A Treasury of Jewish Poetry*, eds. Nathan and Marynn Ausubel (New York: Crown, 1957), 123.

14. Maimonides, *Guide to the Perplexed*, vol. 1, trans. Shlomo Pines (Chicago: University of Chicago Press, 1963), 16–17.

15. Ibid., 18.

16. Ibid., 11–12.

17. Ibid.

18. Alberto Manguel, *A History of Reading* (New York: Penguin Books, 1997), 7.

19. "The Old Man and the Ravishing Maiden" parable is found in the *Zohar*, 2:94b–a, 99a–b, 105, and 114a. It appears here in Daniel Matt's translation in *The Essential Kabbalah* (Edison, NJ: Castle Books, 1995), 141–42.

4. Sarcasm, Tedium, and Transgression

1. Milan Kundera, *Identity*, trans. Linda Asher (New York: Harper Flamingo, 1998), 15.

2. Spacks, *Boredom*, 249.
3. Healy, *Boredom, Self and Culture*, 121.
4. Fromm, *Anatomy of Human Destructiveness*, 272–73.
5. Ibid., 275.
6. Ibid., 278–79.
7. Ibid., 273.
8. Ibid., 275.
9. Aaron Lichtenstein, "To Cultivate and to Guard; The Universal Duties of Mankind," in *By His Light,* ed. Rabbi Reuven Ziegler (Jersey City, NJ: Ktav, 2003), 13.
10. Ibid.
11. David Denby, "Buried Alive: Our Children and the Avalanche of Crud," *New Yorker*, July 15, 1996, 48–51.
12. Svendsen, *Philosophy of Boredom*, 30.
13. Barry Schwartz, *The Paradox of Choice* (New York: Harper Perennial, 2004).

5. Nothing to Do in the Village: Boredom in Community

1. Sebastian de Grazia, *Of Time, Work, and Leisure* (New York: Vintage Books, 1994), 425.
2. See Benedict Anderson's fascinating discussion in *Imagined Communities* (London: Verso, 1991), especially chap. 10, "Census, Map, Museum."
3. W. B. Gallie, "Essentially Contested Concepts," in *Proceedings of the Aristotelian Society*, 1955.
4. Andrew Mason, *Community, Solidarity, and Belonging: Levels of Community and Their Normative Significance* (Cambridge: Cambridge University Press, 2000), 17.
5. For two seminal studies of homophily, see M. McPherson, L. Smith-Lovin, and J. Cook, "Birds of a Feather: Homophily in Social Networks," *Annual Review of Sociology* 27 (2001): 415–44; and P. Lazarsfeld and R. K. Merton, "Friendship as a Social Process: A Substantive and Methodological Analysis," in *Freedom and Control in Modern Society*, eds. Morroe Berger, Theodore Abel, and Charles H. Page (New York: Van Nostrand, 1954), 18–66.
6. De Grazia, *Of Time, Work, and Leisure*, 425.
7. Anthony Storr writes, "It is widely believed that interpersonal relationships of an intimate kind are the chief, if not the only, source of human happiness. Yet the lives of creative individuals often seem to run counter to this assumption" (*Solitude* [New York: Ballentine Books, 1989], ix).
8. Walter Bagehot, *The Collected Works of Walter Bagehot*, ed. Norman St. John-Stevas (London: The Economist, 1965–86), 3:243, quoted in Robert Putnam, *Bowling Alone: The Collapse and Revival of American Community* (New York: Simon & Schuster, 2000), 352.
9. Gary Larson, *The Far Side Gallery* (Kansas City: Andrews and McMeel, 1994), 144.

10. This Jewish law has as its biblical source the story of Hannah from 1 Samuel, where Hannah prays in close physical proximity to Eli but with sufficient distance that he cannot tell what she is doing. He, therefore, accuses her inaccurately of being drunk, when in actuality she was bemoaning her infertility with such anguish that Eli had never seen this intensity of prayer.

11. Erich Fromm, *The Sane Society* (New York: Rinehart, 1955), 61.

12. Ibid., 61.

13. Jonathan Elkins, *Hasidic Wisdom* (Northvale, NJ: Jason Aaronson, 1998), 73.

14. Ibid., 63.

15. Abraham Joshua Heschel, *A Passion for Truth* (New York: Farrar, Straus, and Giroux, 1973), 215.

16. Ibid., 144.

17. Rabbi Joseph Soloveitchik, "The Community," *Tradition* 17, no. 2 (Spring, 1978): 7–24.

18. Fromm observes that not all claims for solitude are genuine: "If an individual claims to be self, an 'I' only for the purpose of differentiating himself from people, from other selves, his claim is nothing but an empty negation, the absence of an image, contrariety. However, individualism implies strong positive content, a matchless unique quality and perspectives, experiences, or events not to be found in any other human being" (*The Sane Society*, e19).

19. Robert Putnam, *Bowling Alone* (New York: Simon & Schuster, 2000), 298.

20. Ibid., 288.

21. Martin Buber, *The Way of Man* (Wallingford, PA: Pendle Hill, 2003), pamphlet 106, 24.

6. Prayer, Habituation, and Holy Insecurity

1. Jack Wertheimer, "The American Synagogue: A House of Boredom, Worship, or What?" in *American Jewish Year Book 2005* (New York: American Jewish Committee, 2005).

2. Sherre Zwelling Hirsch, "Breaking the Boredom Curse," *Jewish Journal* (Los Angeles), September 30, 2005.

3. *Keter Shem Tov* (Jerusalem, 1968), 48a–b; *Sefer Baal Shem Tov* (Sotmar, 1943), 1:122, quoted in Louis Jacobs, *Hasidic Prayer* (London: Littman Library, 1993), 77.

4. Jacobs, *Hasidic Prayer*, 83.

5. See Exodus 34:8, 1 Kings 8:22–23 and 8:54, and Isaiah 1:15 and 45:23 as examples.

6. See M. Wilensky, *Hasidim U-Mitnaggedim* (Jerusalem: Bialik Institute 1970), 2:207.

7. Maimonides, *Mishneh Torah*, "Laws of Prayer," 5:1.

8. Maimonides, *Mishneh Torah*, "Laws of Prayer," chap. 5.

9. Blu Greenberg, *How to Run a Traditional Jewish Household* (New York: Fireside, 1985), 21.

10. William James, *The Varieties of Religious Experience* (Cambridge, MA: Harvard University Press, 1985), 15.
11. Robert C. Fuller, *Wonder: From Emotion to Spirituality* (Chapel Hill: University of North Carolina, 2006), 77.
12. Daniel Gilbert, *Stumbling on Happiness* (New York: Knopf, 2006), 130.
13. Ibid., 131.
14. Shubert Spero, "Is Judaism an Optimistic Religion?" in *A Treasury of "Tradition,"* eds. Norman Lamm and Walter Wurzburger (New York: Hebrew Publishing Company, 1967), 214.
15. This observation was first published on the Internet in *Weekly Jewish Wisdom: Delayed Gratification* by Erica Brown, May 14, 2009, Partnership for Jewish Life and Learning website, www.pjll.org.
16. Jonah Lehrer, "Don't," *New Yorker,* May 18, 2009.

7. Burnt Out in the Jewish Classroom

1. John Berryman, *Seventy-Seven Dream Songs* (New York: Farrar, Straus, and Giroux, 1964), 16.
2. Wendy Mogel, *The Blessing of a Skinned Knee* (New York: Penguin Compass, 2001), 230–31.
3. Healy, *Boredom, Self and Culture,* 129.
4. Ibid., 123.
5. Mari Clayton Glamser, "Notes from a Teacher/Soldier in the Learning Revolution," *Houston Chronicle,* April 19, 1998.
6. Nassim Nicholas Taleb, *The Black Swan: The Impact of the Highly Improbable* (New York: Random House, 2007), 125.
7. Ibid.
8. Healy, *Boredom, Self and Culture,* 121.
9. A useful technique to collect this information is letter writing to the teacher, as described by Susan Handelman in her article "Just as All Their Faces Are Different: The Jewish, the Personal and the Pedagogical." Teachers can also ask students for a list of questions that trouble them at the beginning of a course and write them on the board. The teacher then follows up by giving each student a copy of these questions and showing students where, in the course of their studies, these questions will be further explored.
10. John Holt, *What Do I Do Monday?* (New York: E. P. Dutton, 1970), 68.
11. Michel de Montaigne, *The Complete Essays,* trans. M. A. Screech (London: Penguin, 1991), 2:9, 1109.
12. Healy, *Boredom, Self and Culture,* 131.
13. John Dewey, *Education and Experience* (New York: Collier, 1971), 18–19.
14. Michael Rosenak, *Tree of Life, Tree of Knowledge* (Cambridge, MA: Westview Press, 2001), 111.
15. Ibid.

16. Suzanne K. Langer, quoted in Cynthia Ozick, "Notes toward Finding the Right Question," in *On Being a Jewish Feminist*, ed. Susannah Heschel (New York: Schocken Books, 1983), 120.

8. Boredom and Wonder

1. Winston S. Churchill, *Painting as a Pastime* (New York: Cornerstone Library, 1965), 8–9.
2. Ibid., 7.
3. Ibid., 14.
4. Ibid., 17.
5. Robert C. Fuller, *Wonder: From Emotion to Spirituality* (Chapel Hill: University of North Carolina Press, 2006), 2.
6. Friedrich Nietzsche, *The Gay Science* (New York: Random House, 1974), 296.
7. Fuller, *Wonder*, 9.
8. Ibid., 9.
9. Maimonides, *Mishneh Torah*, "Laws of Idol Worship," chap. 1.
10. Ibid., 1:3.
11. Fuller, *Wonder*, 12.
12. Bahya ibn Pakuda, *Hovot Ha-Levavot, Shaar Ha-Yihud*, 7.
13. Abraham Isaiah Karelitz, *Emunot U'bitahon* 1:7, quoted in Natan Slifkin, *Man and Beast* (Brooklyn: Zoo Torah, 2006), 22. I changed his translation for ease of reading.
14. Fuller, *Wonder*, 15.
15. As told by Aaron Rakeffet-Rothkoff, *The Rav* (New York: Ktav, 1999), 2:165–66.
16. Ibid, 169.
17. This entire discussion takes place in the Babylonian Talmud, *Berakhot* 53a.
18. *Mishnah Berurah* 217:1–1.
19. Abraham Joshua Heschel, *God in Search of Man* (New York: Farrar, Strauss, and Giroux, 1976), 45.
20. Ibid, 45.
21. Ibid, 46.
22. Ibid, 46.
23. Louis Jacobs, *Jewish Thought Today* (New York: Behrman House, 1970), 10–11.
24. Diane Ackerman, *A Natural History of the Senses* (New York: Vintage Books, 1990), 304–5.
25. Norman Lamm, *Faith and Doubt* (New York: Ktav, 1986), 203.
26. Ibid., 203–4.
27. Joseph Pieper, *Leisure: The Basis of Culture* (New York: Random House, 1963), 42–54.

28. Arnold Posy, "Belief in Judaism in a Generation of Disbelief," in *Great Yiddish Writers of the Twentieth Century*, ed. Joseph Leftwich (Northvale, NJ: Jason Aronson, 1987), 661.
29. Ibid., 663.
30. James Elkins, *Pictures and Tears* (New York: Routledge, 2001), 210.
31. Ibid., 248.
32. Abraham Isaac Kook, *Orot Ha-Kodesh* 2:517, quoted in Matt, *The Essential Kabbalah* (Edison, NJ: Castle Books, 1995), 99.

9. Boredom and Authenticity

1. "Boredom Hurts—The 2008 Ford Escape Is the Cure," Ford, www.boredomhurts.com (2008).
2. Erich Fromm, *Man for Himself: An Inquiry into the Psychology of Ethics* (New York: Macmillan, 1990), 40.
3. Jonathan Sacks, *Celebrating Life* (London: Continuum Books, 2000), 172–3.
4. Healy, *Boredom, Self and Culture*, 87–88.
5. Richard Winter, *Still Bored in a Culture of Entertainment* (Downers Grove, IL: InterVarsity Press, 2002), 137.
6. Healy, *Boredom, Self and Culture*, 121.
7. Maimonides, *Mishneh Torah*, "Laws of Repentance," 2:4. He mentions there that moving to a new area creates humility, ostensibly because a person has to establish himself anew and cannot rely upon old connections or prior knowledge.
8. Abraham Isaac Kook, "Lights of Penitence," trans. Ben Zion Bokser, in *Abraham Isaac Kook* (New York: Paulist Press, 1978), 56.
9. Ibid., 56.
10. Ibid., 156.
11. Arnold Band, *Nahman of Bratslav: The Tales* (New York: Paulist Press, 1978). The story "The *Hakham* and the *Tam*" is found on pages 131–138.
12. Ibid. See Band's commentary, 309.
13. Emile Durkheim, *Suicide*, 2:6, section 1 (1897, trans. 1951).
14. Heschel, *Passion for Truth*, 129.
15. Luzzatto, *Path of the Just*, 76–77.
16. Ibid., 89–91.
17. Heschel, *Passion for Truth*, 143.
18. Logan Pearsall Smith, *The English Language* (London: Oxford University Press, 1966), 128, quoted in Healy, *Boredom, Self and Culture*, 24.
19. Healy, *Boredom, Self and Culture*, 24.
20. Dov Katz, *Tenuat Ha-Mussar* (Tel-Aviv: Beitan Ha-Sefer, 1946), 269.
21. Alain de Botton, *How Proust Can Change Your Life*, 3.
22. Martin Buber, *The Tales of Rabbi Nachman* (New York: Horizon Press, 1956), 37.
23. Joan Didion, *The Year of Magical Thinking* (New York: Vintage, 2007), 1.
24. Diane Ackerman, *Natural History of the Senses*, 301.

25. Soloveitchik, in Rakeffet-Rothkoff, *The Rav*, 167–68.
26. Erich Fromm, *Psychoanalysis and Religion* (New York: Oxford University Press, 1998), 60.
27. Robert Nozick, *The Examined Life* (New York: Simon & Schuster, 1989), 132.
28. Blaise Pascal, *Pensees* (New York: Penguin, 1995), section 8, diversion #136, 37.
29. Adin Steinsaltz, *The Thirteen Petalled Rose* (New York: Basic Books, 2006), 107–9.
30. Nozick, *The Examined Life*, 128.
31. Ackerman, *Natural History of the Senses*, 309.

10. An End to Boredom—Some Practical Advice

1. Arthur Green, *Seek My Face: A Jewish Mystical Theology* (Woodstock, VT: Jewish Lights, 2006), 29.
2. Benedict Carey, "You're Checked Out, but Your Brain Is Tuned In," *New York Times,* August 5, 2008, www.nytimes.com/2008/08/05/health/research/05mind.html.
3. Ibid.
4. Russell, *Conquest of Happiness*, 48.
5. Ibid., 48–49.
6. Ibid., 49.
7. Ibid., 50.
8. Ibid., 52.
9. Ibid., 51.
10. Susan Cosio, "A Daily Walk Just to Listen" in *This I Believe,* eds. Jay Allison and Dan Gediman (New York: Holt, 2007), 44.
11. Eric Wilson, *Against Happiness* (New York: Farrar, Straus, and Giroux, 2008), 81.
12. "Commencement; Dartmouth College," *New York Times,* June 12, 1989, http://query.nytimes.com/gst/fullpage.html?res=950DE5DA163DF931A257 55C0A96F948. I am grateful to Adam Lehman, who shared this source with me after first hearing it as his own graduation. It was a message that clearly stayed with him long after his graduation, when so many commencement addresses are quickly forgotten.
13. Ibid.
14. Ibid.
15. From the *Additional Service for Rosh Hashanah,* trans. Avraham Davis, *The Metzudah Machzor Rosh Hashanah* (New York: Noble Book, 1982), 341–42.
16. Raposa, *Boredom and the Religious Imagination,* 3.
17. John Gardner, "Personal Renewal," in *Western Journal of Medicine* 157 (October, 1992): 457–59.
18. Daniel C. Matt, *The Essential Kabbalah,* 67. Translation of Asher ben David cited by Ephraim Gottlieb, *Ha-Qabbalah be-Khitvei Rabbenu Bahya ben Asher* (Jerusalem: Kiryath Sepher, 1970), 84.

Printed in the USA
CPSIA information can be obtained
at www.ICGtesting.com
JSHW012030140824
68134JS00033B/2967

9 781683 363088